Academy of ....

AHA German Longsword Study Guide

Authors:
Keith Farrell
Alex Bourdas

1ˢᵗ Edition
28ᵗʰ August 2013
ISBN 978-0-9926735-0-5
Published by Fallen Rook Publishing

The Academy of Historical Arts and Fallen Rook Publishing are divisions within Triquetra Services (Scotland), a charitable organisation registered in Scotland: registration number SC042086.

Version and Copyright Information

Version: 1st Edition
Date: 28th August 2013
Copyright © Keith Farrell, 2013
Copyright © Alex Bourdas, 2013
ISBN 978-0-9926735-0-5

Note about Illustrations

The illustrations in this book have been hand-drawn by Alex Bourdas, inspired by the original works, then scanned to electronic format and cleaned up with some additional editing help from Keith Farrell and Daria Izdebska. The book cover has been designed by Daria Izdebska.

Publisher

This book has been published by Fallen Rook Publishing, a division of Triquetra Services (Scotland), which is a charity registered in Scotland with number SC042086; published in Glasgow, United Kingdom, in August 2013.

CHAPTER 4: GUARDS 32

CHAPTER 5: STRIKES   53

Acknowledgements

I would like to thank several people for their help and inspiration during this project.

My co-author Alex Bourdas has been invaluable; the research and understandings would not have developed as quickly without his help. My good friend and colleague Ben Kerr gave me my first introduction to the concept of historical European martial arts, so without his input, this project would never have begun! Another very important person is Andreas Engström, without whom I would never have begun to work on translating any of the sources.

Two people who have really challenged me to improve my physical abilities as well as my theoretical knowledge of the subject are Tim Gallagher and Mark Wilkie. Without the constant challenge provided by these two skilful gentlemen I would not have been pushed to become anywhere near as skilful, and would not have had the opportunity to develop my understanding of the more complex concepts of the art.

I would also like to thank Daria Izdebska for putting up with me for so many mornings, afternoons and evenings as I typed away at this manuscript, for listening patiently to my many ideas, and for reminding me to do things like eating and sleeping from time to time. And then of course, thanks are due for her frantic efforts to proofread the book and to help with the editing just before I put the manuscript to print. The book that you hold in your hands right how would be much poorer without her input, and I am very grateful for her efforts and advice.

Keith Farrell
7th August 2013

Foreword (a.k.a. "why we have written this book")

Alex and I began working on this book in the September of 2010, with the intention of creating a brief but comprehensive study guide for use within the Academy of Historical Arts. The scope of the project ballooned from there, becoming more ambitious, until it matured into this textbook.

When I was first introduced to historical European martial arts in late 2008, my exposure was to Mike Rasmusson's translation of Talhoffer's manuscript from 1467 and to Grzegorz Żabiński's translation of the *Codex Wallerstein*. These works were interesting, but obscure, and the teaching of the subject in Scotland at that time was enthusiastic but not pedagogically sound or effective. With a lot of background in karate, and with some experience with Viking age re-enactment, I was able to handle a sword to some extent; albeit not properly, and not particularly well, but my karate experience gave me the edge I needed to win most of my sparring bouts. When people tried to use the tricks from Talhoffer and the *Codex Wallerstein* against me, the tricks simply didn't work, and so I became quite biased against what I saw as an inadequate and ineffective system of fighting.

However, in the summer of 2010, I decided that since there were quite a lot of treatises for German longsword, perhaps there might be something valuable within them if only the material could be found and understood properly – and then taught in a competent fashion. So I read David Lindholm's translation of the *Hs.3227a* and my eyes were opened! This historical source was not particularly clear about how to do anything, but the description of the principles underlying the system made a lot of sense. If only my first exposure had been to a source with a system built from sensible principles, and not to two separate collections of random tricks!

From there, I decided that the best way for me to learn about German longsword was not to take instruction from other people (since that meant either working from Talhoffer and *Codex Wallerstein*, or continuing to learn methods of performing techniques that were ineffective and that could be countered without breaking a sweat); rather, I needed to look into the sources myself, and come to my own understanding of the system. I asked Alex if he would be interested in helping with this project and he agreed to join the effort.

In the three years since we began this project, Alex and I have read far too many treatises, essays and blog articles; we have watched far too many videos on YouTube and participated in all too many forum discussion threads. However, as a result, we have maintained a constant growth in our understanding of the art and have been refining our interpretations and skills consistently. I would not presume to say that our current understanding is perfect, in fact I fully expect that something will change before this book even makes it to print (such is life), but the understanding to which we have come now is reasonably complete and comprehensive.

We could easily continue to research the subject for another two and a half years, but then this book would never become published. There comes a time when every project must call a halt and deliver what results have been achieved, and for this project, the time is now. We can always follow up with further editions or complementary books and DVDs; our Encased in Steel blog is a wonderful resource where thoughts and ideas are posted on a regular basis. By choosing to round off our work on this book now and bring it to publication, we will at least be able to make available the research that has been done so far so that it does not languish away where only Alex and I can see it. Hopefully, people will be able to benefit from the research that we have done so far, and at the very least this book will stand testament to the countless hours of work that Alex and I have poured into researching this particular discipline.

So in the interests of bringing this project to a close, I shall sign off, and add only that I look forward to publishing further books and DVDs on the subject to supplement the groundwork that has been laid by this book!

Sincerely,

Keith Farrell
Senior Instructor
Academy of Historical Arts
Triquetra Services (Scotland)
Registered Charity (SC042086)

Chapter 1: Introduction

Originally, this book was written for students of the Academy of Historical Arts; as the project grew and developed, the scope expanded, and now we believe that many people involved with the study of historical European martial arts will find the work helpful in their own studies. The intention is to make available the research undertaken by Keith Farrell and Alex Bourdas so that others may benefit from the work that has been done to understand the subject and to make it more accessible.

The book is not intended as a "how to" manual. Written word is not a good medium for transferring information about the subject; the historical sources do an excellent job, but modern DVDs and video clips are a much more effective medium for transferring information and teaching martial arts skills. Further publications will address this and will provide "how to" manuals, but this book is not intended to be such a work.

Scholars and students looking to begin their studies in the historical sources may find this book of most benefit. Anyone looking to supplement their practice with reading research on what the historical sources say about techniques, guards and concepts will also find this book to be of some value.

People looking for top quality translations or ground breaking cutting-edge research will sadly not find it in this book. This book is a record of the studies that Keith and Alex have conducted on the topic so far, and is merely a milestone in the continuing path of studying the art.

If you would like to find out more about how the authors have developed their understanding of the art, and to see the sources and rationale behind this understanding, then this book will be helpful.

The general approach to this research can be summarised very briefly:

1) we knew nothing;
2) we looked at some sources;
3) we developed an understanding of what the sources said;
4) we tried to integrate it with our overall understanding of the art;
5) we returned to step 2 and went through it all again.

This has been a very iterative process, with every step forward supported by at least one of the historical sources. We have tried to remain unbiased in the writing of this book, trying to show what the sources say, rather than pushing our own biases and opinions upon readers. At any point in our research, when we found that we were diverging from what the sources said, we brought our approach back in line with the sources and tried to keep the integrity of our research on track.

The first step of the work was to build a glossary of the different terms in the system. This was quite a bit harder than it sounds, because so many of the sources use different terms and different spellings. We have chosen to use the spellings from Ringeck's *MS Dresden C487* as often as possible in order to provide consistency throughout the work.

The next step was to list all the different guard positions, then find what all the sources had to say about them. This was also very difficult, since some guards have so many variations. Vom Tag is a particularly confusing guard if you want to define precisely how it is to be held, so we decided to list all the variations. As a result, the chapter that discusses the guard positions has become a very valuable resource to compare and contrast how different sources describe and display the guards.

Next came the strikes. Again, "nice and simple" one might think, but in reality very difficult! How to describe the attacks in such a way that does not just copy and paste what the historical sources say? Here we decided that a brief summary of the techniques would be most helpful, so that students could see roughly what the term means and how the strike might be done, with regard to the sources, without being exposed to a "one true way" of performing any strike. The chapter about striking is quite a useful reference piece for people who need a helping hand to remember the different strikes and techniques in the system.

Next came our investigation of ranges and timing. This was originally a very easy section write, and then we realised that we had completely misunderstood everything! We went back to the treatises for further study, several times, and eventually developed an understanding of the issue that fits with what the sources both say and imply. This chapter of the book will be most useful for people who know the basics and who would like to put their knowledge of techniques into more advanced context.

The chapter on stance, footwork and grip was an interesting section to write. We went back and forth on this one: sometimes it was easy, then it became difficult, then a lightbulb went off in our heads and it became easy again, then something else made it confusing... Eventually we had to settle for the fact that the sources really don't say much about this issue, but since we had done quite a lot of study on the topic, we provided as much information as we could along with our points of view on the subject. This chapter may be quite helpful for beginners.

Eventually, we decided that we had to make an end to the project somewhere, so we took all the material that we have been working on for the last two years and edited it together into a cohesive volume on the subject. There are certainly some important things missing from this book, and some historical sources have not been touched upon as much as would be ideal, but if we did not call a halt to the research part of the project then the book would never materialise.

We would like to have included more information from the works by Paulus Mair and Joachim Meyer in this book, along with other interesting sources such as the anonymous *MS Best.7020* and the treatise by Hans Medel. We could have included more by Meyer, but without access to the translation by Dr Forgeng and without the opportunity to spend any time studying Meyer's work, it seemed most honest to leave it out of this book. Our intention is to work on Meyer's treatise when we gain access to a good translation, and to release supplementary information in the future once we can make a worthwhile and honest study of the source. For these reasons, this book is most valuable to students of the earlier sources within the Liechtenauer tradition, although students of the later sources may find it interesting to see how the tradition developed through time.

Finally, throughout this book, we often use the pronoun "he" to refer to a combatant. We acknowledge that there are a lot of female combatants studying HEMA, but due to the lack of a suitable gender-neutral pronoun in the English language, we have chosen to refer to combatants with male pronouns to avoid the clumsy "he/she" and "his/her" constructions. We believe such politically correct constructions would obstruct the flow of reading the text and so we have made this choice for aesthetic, practical and space-saving reasons. Our apologies in advance to anyone who feels that this decision was not the correct course of action.

Chapter 2: Preparatory Information

This chapter will provide some preparatory information about the sword itself and about the Liechtenauer tradition that will be studied as the subject of this book.

2.1 Parts of the Longsword

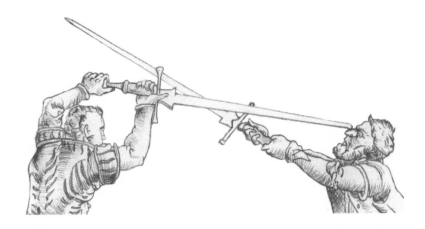

2.1.1 Schwert - Sword

Schwert is the German word for sword. The longsword was sometimes referred to as the "langes schwert"[1] to differentiate it from other types of sword.

2.1.2 Ort - Point

The point is the very tip of the blade and is used for thrusts.

2.1.3 Schneide - Edge

The longsword has a two-edged blade, with both edges sharpened for slices and strikes.

---

[1] Sigmund ain Ringeck. *MS Dresden C487*, c.1504-19 (trans. Keith Farrell, 2011), 10v.

2.1.4 Lange Schneide - Long Edge

The long edge is the edge facing the same direction as the swordsman's knuckles; when holding the sword with the arms straight out in front of the body, the long edge of the sword is the edge that is pointing away from the swordsman.

2.1.5 Kurze Schneide - Short Edge

The short edge is the edge facing the other direction from the swordsman's knuckles; when holding the sword with the arms straight out in front of the body, the short edge of the sword is the edge that is pointing back towards the swordsman.

2.1.6 Hohlkehle - Fuller

This is the groove down the blade. Some swords had a fuller and some swords did not. It had the purpose of lightening the blade while maintaining strength along the edges. Under no circumstances was it ever a "blood groove"; this idea is merely modern nonsense.

2.1.7 Klinge - Blade

The blade of the sword was made from high quality steel. Some blades were forged with a fuller down the centre to lighten the weight; other blades were constructed with a diamond cross-section to allow for easier and more effective thrusts. A researcher called Ewart Oakeshott created a typology of different blade shapes, based on his studies of several swords from museums and collections across the world.[2]

2.1.8 Schilt - Shield

The schilt is a protruding section at the base of the blade, just above the crossguard. This can perform various functions, including improving the balance and handling of the sword and protecting the fingers.

2.1.9 Gehilze - Crossguard / Quillons

The crossguard is the horizontal guard between the grip and the blade. Its purpose is to help protect a swordsman's fingers from an opponent's sword sliding down the blade. The crossguard is also sometimes known as the quillons.

---

[2] Ewart Oakeshott. *Records of the Medieval Sword* (The Boydell Press, 1991).

2.1.10 Klos - Pommel

The pommel is the solid counterweight at the bottom of the hilt that brings the balance point of the weapon closer to the grip. Without the effect of the pommel the weapon would be much less balanced and more difficult to wield.

> For the sword is like a scale: if the sword is large and heavy, then the pommel must likewise be large and heavy, so that it will balance like a scale.[3]

The pommel could also be used offensively, in pommel strikes. Furthermore, if it could be unscrewed, it could also be thrown at an opponent, as seen in the *Gladiatoria*.[4]

2.1.11 Heft - Grip

The grip is where the swordsman should hold the weapon with both hands.

2.1.12 Starke - Strong

The strong of the blade is the lower half of the blade, the half that is closer to the hilt.

2.1.13 Schwech - Weak

The weak of the blade is the upper half of the blade, the half that is further from the hilt.

2.2 Masters within the Liechtenauer Tradition

The Liechtenauer Tradition is a long tradition of fencing that was started by a man called Johannes Liechtenauer. Unfortunately, we have very little information about Liechtenauer himself, but we are told in the *Hs.3227a* that he spent many years travelling, learning under different masters, in "many lands." The source tells us:

> The sword has but one art, which was devised and developed centuries ago. This art is the foundation and core of fighting, and Master Liechtenauer knew and understood it completely. He did not devise or develop the art, but rather he journeyed and searched through many lands in his quest to learn and understand this art.[5]

---

[3] Anonymous. *Hs.3227a*, c.1389 (rendered into English by Keith Farrell, 2013, informed by the translations of: Lindholm, Żabiński, Wallhausen, Hull, Kleinau and Stoeppler), 15r.
[4] Anonymous. *MS KK5013*, c.1430, 7r.
[5] Anonymous. *Hs.3227a*, (trans. Keith Farrell, 2013), 13v.

Thus the earliest source about Liechtenauer proclaims that he did not invent the art of fighting, or Kunst des Fechten (often shortened to KDF by modern practitioners), by himself. However, he did apparently have a complete understanding of the art of fighting and summarised his knowledge in his verses on unarmoured combat with the longsword,[6] fighting from horseback,[7] and fighting on foot in armour.[8] These verses, while succinct, are hard to understand by themselves, and so many later masters would go on to write glosses of his verses in order to explain them.

The first of these glosses is the *Hs.3227a*, which is traditionally dated to 1389, although we cannot be certain that this date is correct.[9] The *Hs.3227a* is often referred to as having been written by Hanko Döbringer, but there is no evidence that Döbringer wrote the codex. In fact, Döbringer's name is only mentioned in a short section that deals with the teachings of masters other than Liechtenauer.

The next glosses appear in the *Codex 44.A.8* (often referred to today as the *Codex Danzig* after Peter von Danzig) and in the *Codex I.6.4°.3* (often referred to as the *Codex Lew*, after Jud Lew). In both these cases, Peter von Danzig and Jud Lew only authored one section out of several contained within their respective codices.

The *Codex 44.A.8* is internally dated to 1452,[10] and the *Codex I.6.4°.3* is dated to the 1450s.[11] It is unclear why there is such a long gap in time between the *Hs.3227a* and these two manuscripts, with around 60 years between the *Hs.3227a* and the next fight-books to mention Liechtenauer by name. This is not to say that there were no German fight-books produced in the period of roughly 60 years between those manuscripts, as authors such as Hans Talhoffer produced manuscripts in this period and some manuscripts by the Gladiatoria group came into being in the first half of the 15th century. These manuscripts, however, do not mention Liechtenauer by name. It is also worth noting that the treatises contained in the *Codex 44.A.8* and in the *Codex I.6.4°.3* may have been written before the codices were compiled in the 1450s and that the codices contain copies of earlier texts; it may just be the case that these are the first surviving copies of the treatises.

---

[6] Also known as Blossfechten, Bloszfechten or Bloßfechten.

[7] Also known as Rossfechten, Roszfechten or Roßfechten.

[8] Also known as Harnischfechten.

[9] Christian Tobler. *In St George's Name* (Freelance Academy Press, 2010).

[10] Anonymous. *Codex 44.A.8*, 1452, 113v.

[11] Grzegorz Żabiński. *The Longsword Teachings of Master Liechtenauer. The Early Sixteenth Century Swordsmanship Comments in the "Goliath" Manuscript (Adam Marshall, 2010).*

In 1470, Paulus Kal wrote the *CGM 1507*, in which he included a list of the members of the Society of Liechtenauer. It appears that this was an honorific for dead masters who belonged to the Liechtenauer tradition, and it included two types of authors: men who had written glosses of Liechtenauer's verses, and men who had written their own material. We have treatises by some of the masters listed by Kal, but some of them either did not write treatises or their treatises have since been lost.

Among the masters of the Society of Liechtenauer, those few from whom we have surviving treatises are: Peter von Danzig; Andres Lignitzer; Sigmund Amring; Martin Huntfeltz; Ott Jud.

Peter von Danzig's name literally means Peter from Danzig; a city that is now known as Gdańsk and is located in modern Poland. Peter von Danzig wrote a gloss of Liechtenauer's armoured combat.

Andres Lignitzer was from Liegnitz, which today is known as Legnica, and is also in modern Poland. Andres Lignitizer is credited with writing treatises on wrestling, dagger, armoured combat and sword and buckler. In addition to this, a short treatise comparing the messer and the longsword is found in the *MS M.I.29* and was written by a Master Andreas, who may or may not be the same person as Andres Lignitzer.[12] Finally, someone called Andres Juden is mentioned in the *Hs.3227a*. Andres Juden means Andres the Jew, and again this may or may not be the same person as Andres Lignitzer.

Modern practitioners and researchers most commonly refer to Sigmund Amring as Sigmund Ringeck, but he is referred to by a number of different names in the manuscripts: Sigmund Amring,[13] Sigmund Emring,[14] Sigmund Schining,[15] Sigmundt Einring,[16] and Sigmund ain Ringeck.[17] The name most commonly used by modern practitioners seems to be a shortening of Sigmund ain Ringeck. He wrote commentaries on all three sections of Liechtenauer's art (armoured and unarmoured longsword, and mounted combat). He also added some of his own longsword teachings to his gloss of Liechtenauer's unarmed longsword fencing, in which he offers detail on how to fence using Nebenhut, Schrankhut, Lang Ort, and also how to use a few additional counters. He was the "fencing master to the highborn prince and noble Lord Albrecht, Count Palatine of Rhine and Duke of Bavaria."[18]

Martin Huntfeltz was another very prolific writer in the society. He produced works on dagger, armoured combat and mounted combat. He may have come from the village of Hündsfeld, in what is now central Germany.

---

[12] Keith Farrell. "The pedagogical skill of Andre Lignitzer, a 15th century fencing master." *Katsujinken, a Sword Arts Journal* 5, (2013): 12-15.

[13] Paulus Kal. *CGM 1507*, c.1470, 2r.

[14] Sigmund Emring. *E.1939.65.341*, 1508, 22r.

[15] Sigmund Shining. *Codex I.6.2º.5*, c.1560, 21r.

[16] Sigmundt Einring. *MS Var.82*, c.1570, 6r.

[17] Ringeck. *MS Dresden C487*, 11r.

[18] Ibid.

The last of these individuals, Ott Jud, or Ott the Jew, is described as the wrestling master to the lords of Austria.[19] He produced a wrestling treatise that is contained in many manuscripts such as the *Codex Ringeck*,[20] the *Codex Danzig*,[21] one of Talhoffer's manuscripts,[22] and many more.

The writings of Liechtenauer and his society were so influential that as late as 1571, they were still being re-used in manuals. In 1571, Joachim Meyer compiled the *Fechtbüch zu Ross und zu Fuss* (*MS Var.82*), in which he included treatises written by Sigmund Schining ain Ringeck, Martin Syber, Jud Lew, Martin Huntfeltz, Andres Lignitzer, as well as his own treatise on the rappier, a weapon which is often referred to as the "side sword" today (and is not precisely the same as the rapier).

In 1570, just a year before this, Meyer completed his *Gründtliche Beschreibung der Kunst des Fechtens*, a huge and well-detailed book full of his own unique material. A lot of this material lies outside the Liechtenauer tradition, but is very valuable to practitioners who study 16th century German longsword.

Few fight-books were produced in the Liechtenauer tradition after this, and all of them were written entirely by a single author, rather than being compendiums of various treatises, as many of the earlier manuals were.

In 1612, Jakob Sutor wrote the penultimate treatise in the Liechtenauer tradition, the *New Kůnstliches Fechtbuch*. This manual showed less attention to the traditional weapon of the Liechtenauer tradition, the longsword, in favour of the rappier. Following this, the Liechtenauer tradition seemed to be at least partially ousted by imported Italian methods, as shown in the fight-books of Sebastian Heussler, or Hans Wilhelm Schoeffer, who both show a heavy Italian influence.

---

[19] Ott Jud. *Codex 44.A.8*, 1452 100v.
[20] Ott Jud. *MS Dresden C487*, c.1504-19, 78r-85r.
[21] Ott Jud. *Codex 44.A.8*, 1452, 100v-107v.
[22] Ott Jud. *MS Chart.A.558*, 1443, 109v-114v.

Finally, in 1679, Theodor Verolini produced the final treatise in the Liechtenauer tradition, *Der Künstliche Fechter*. This treatise, as far as we know, represents the historic end of the Liechtenauer tradition, up until its modern day revival.

2.3 Fight-books and Manuscripts

There were many fight-books (fechtbücher) produced between the 14th and early 17th centuries on the subject of the German longsword. Some fencing masters wrote many works; some masters wrote but a single book, some authors merely compiled the works of earlier masters into new fight-books. Yet other masters may well have written fight-books that have since become lost... It can be very confusing to a new student of the discipline to hear all of the names of the different masters and fight-books, so for more information, the authors can do no better than to suggest reading the Wiktenauer for a comprehensive and well-researched overview of the subject: http://www.wiktenauer.com/

2.4 Essay: Length of the Longsword

by Alex Bourdas

When buying a new weapon, you must think about the length of the weapon, in addition to price, weight, balance etc. If your weapon is too long, then it will become unwieldy, and if it is too short, you may struggle to execute some techniques correctly.

Unfortunately, none of the masters within the KDF tradition gave any explicit instructions for how long a sword should be. Other masters in other styles, such as Silver and Vadi, did provide instruction on how to work out the ideal length of your sword. Examining the lengths of surviving swords from the period at random may also be misleading, as one may need to account for a difference in height between the medieval and the modern man, and there is no guarantee that any one particular surviving sword would have been appropriate for use in the Liechtenauer tradition.

There have been some articles discussing the need for longer swords, and advancing the notion that modern sparring swords are too short.[23] While I believe there is some truth to this idea, I also believe that most modern swords are of an acceptable length, even if they are on the short side, and I intend to show this by looking at the length of the sword presented in the artwork of the fight-books.

---

[23] Roger Norling. "How long should a longsword be?" *HROARR*, 2011. http://www.hroarr.com/how-long-should-a-longsword-be/

To this end, here is a list of several of the major illustrated treatises, comparing the ratios of the height of the people depicted to the total length of the swords, and also the ratios of height to length of blade. To form these ratios, I picked four plates from each manuscript, calculated a separate ratio for "height to total length" and "height to blade length" for each of those four plates, and finally averaged them. This provided the average of these two separate ratios for each manuscript.

Illustrated Treatise	Ratio of height to total length	Ratio of height to blade length
Codex Wallerstein (part C), c.1430	0.90	0.67
Hans Talhoffer, 1467	0.83	0.62
Paulus Kal, 1470	0.69	0.55
Codex Wallerstein (part A), c.1470	0.76	0.55
Peter Falkner, 1495	0.71	0.52
Glasgow Fechtbüch, 1508	0.79	0.56
Goliath, c.1510	0.96	0.69
Andre Paurñfeyndt, 1516	0.83	0.56
Hans Medel, 1539	0.87	0.65
Paulus Mair, c.1542	0.77	0.60
Jörg Wilhalm Hutter, 1564	0.85	0.59
Joachim Meyer, 1570	0.83	0.59

Table 1 - ratios from treatise illustrations

Basically, what these numbers mean is that an average height to total length ratio can be anywhere between 0.69 and 0.96.

My height is 5 foot 9, or 69 inches; so this means that if I use these ratios, my longsword should have a total length of anywhere around 47.6 to 66.2 inches, and the blade length should be roughly between 35.9 and 47.6 inches.

For a complete list of total and blades lengths calculated for a variety of different heights, please see the "Longsword Lengths" handout by Jonathan Allen. [24] The handout was based the information presented above, and expanded upon the table.

If we look at a few of the more commonly used longsword trainers, we can see that most of them actually fit within the specifications derived from my height.

Sword type	Total length	Blade length
A&A Fechterspiel	48.50"	37.75"
A&A Spada da Zogho	46.50"	35.75"
Albion Liechtenauer	47.50"	36.50"
Albion Meyer	47.75"	36.50"
Cold Steel Hand-and-a-Half Training Sword	44.00"	34.00"
Hanwei Practical Bastard Sword	49.50"	38.00"
Hanwei Practical Hand-and-a-Half Sword	43.75"	34.00"
Rawlings Synthetic Sparring Longsword	48.50"	38.00"
Tinker Pearce Longsword	47.25"	35.25"

Table 2 - lengths of swords

So out of this list, it is only the Hanwei Practical Hand-and-a-Half and the Cold Steel Hand-and-a-Half that are too small. Some of the swords might not quite match the ratios in Table 1 above, but they are close enough. The total length of the Spada da Zogho is only 0.9 inches shorter than my lowest total length estimate, which isn't particularly important, especially bearing in mind that the numbers are just estimates, not hard and fast rules. The manuscript art gives us a rough indication of how long the swords should be, but they were not drawn exactly so that a few hundred years later someone could measure them to the nearest millimetre. So a sword not exactly matching the ratios above isn't a massive problem, as long as the ratios are reasonably close. I would argue that the Hanwei and Cold Steel Hand-and-a-Half swords are too short, but that all the other training swords mentioned above are fine in terms of length, at least for me.

---

[24] Jonathan Allen. "Longsword Lengths." *Grauenwolf*, 2012.
http://grauenwolf.files.wordpress.com/2012/11/longsword-lengths3.pdf

It is worth noting that for the purpose of this essay, I define the longsword simply as a sword that is designed so that it can be used with two hands on the grip. For an example of a different approach, see Richard Marsden's essay "The longsword as a battlefield weapon" where he argues that the longsword and the two handed sword are intrinsically different weapons.[25] This is not something I personally agree with, although there is some historical evidence for a separation of the two.

Joseph Swetnam wrote about weapons (or perhaps more accurately, styles of fighting used with those weapons) that are derived from the sword and from the rapier. From the sword, he wrote, is derived "the two hand sword" as well as "the bastard sword, the which Sword is some-thing shorter than a long Sword, and yet longer than a Short-sword".[26]

The London Masters of Defence also categorised the long sword, the bastard sword, and the two handed sword as different weapons, with the long sword being by far the most popular of the three.[27]

However, there is no evidence that different methods of use for longswords, two-handed swords, and bastard swords were distinguished between in the Liechtenauer tradition. Andre Paurñfeyndt wrote about "how one should use advantage in the longsword, which will be used with both hands, as the battle sword, riding sword, estoc, and many others, which I will for brevity's sake leave out".[28] This suggests that within the KDF tradition, a variety of different swords, possibly of different lengths, can all be used in the same manner.

It may be worth experimenting with swords of differing lengths to find what dimensions are most comfortable, but as long as a sword fits within the rough guidelines mentioned above, it would likely be of an acceptable length for use within KDF.

[25] Richard Marsden. "The longsword as a battlefield weapon." *The Works of Richard Marsden*, 2011. http://www.worksofrichardmarsden.com/historyofthelongsword.htm

[26] Joseph Swetnam. *The Schoole of the Noble and Worthy Science of Defence*, 1617, chapter XII.

[27] John Dylan Murray. "Prizes of the London Masters of Defense" *Iceweasel.org*, 1998. http://iceweasel.org/lmod_analysis.html

[28] Andre Paurñfeyndt. *Ergrundung Ritterlicher Kunst der Fechterey*, 1516 (trans. Kevin Maurer), A3r.

Chapter 3: Stance, Footwork, Grip

This chapter will look at the issues of stance, footwork and how to grip the sword. These issues often seem inconsequential beside the more interesting and "difficult" concepts of technical interpretation and cutting mechanics, but they are nonetheless very important to a complete study of the art.

3.1 Stance: Height, Weight and Body Alignment

Here we are going to distinguish between the two terms "stance" and "guard." The term "stance" will be used to refer to body positioning, while the term "guard" will refer to the position of the sword in relation to the body.

One's stance is determined by two characteristics: height and weight. Height refers to how high or low a stance is held and weight refers to how the weight of one's body is distributed between the legs. All stances are assumed to be balanced positions with a reasonable height and weight, because if a combatant is not balanced then he might fall over.

3.1.1 How high or low should one stand while in stance?

None of the medieval fencing masters discuss the ideal height for stances in any detail in the surviving manuscripts. The illustrations of combatants in the surviving manuscripts can provide some clues as to how deeply one should sit in stance while fighting, but may not be able to provide a definitive answer. Another valuable question is why the height of stance is important, and this question is worth answering first.

Some martial arts teach a very high stance where the feet are fairly close together, others teach a slightly wider stance, and yet other arts teach very deep and low stances. This is because different martial arts have different purposes; they are designed to solve different problems in terms of how the fighting is to take place. On the one hand, Freestyle and Graeco-Roman wrestling often teach deep stances, because the purpose is to make the body well grounded in order to prevent takedowns. On the other hand, taekwondo and some styles of kung fu often teach some higher stances, because these styles favour kicks, and it is much more difficult to kick from a low grounded stance than from a higher stance. This shows that different arts require different stances, which leads to the question: what kind of stance is most appropriate to the German longsword?

A handful of manuscripts show combatants with a high stance where the legs are almost straight and where the back is held in a very upright fashion. The feet can be very close together, sometimes even touching. Some of the illustrations in manuscripts by Paulus Kal and Hans Talhoffer show this type of stance, although not all of the works by these masters show this type of stance.[29] The *Glasgow Fechtbüch* also shows some high stances.[30] What the *Glasgow Fechtbüch* has in common with the earliest of Talhoffer's works and the earlier works by Kal is that occasionally the artwork is not well executed, and so the high stance could merely be a product of inferior drawing ability on the part of the artist, or alternatively it could be a stylistic effect. In any case, this does not seem to be a style of stance that appears often in the manuscripts, and certainly not in any of the works with high levels of detail in the artwork.

Most of the manuscripts show a more balanced middle stance in which the knees are bent comfortably, taking the body's centre of gravity reasonably low as if the combatants were preparing for some kind of springing motion. This is the stance from which most longsword fencers will fight naturally after a little training, as it is the most natural way to stand when preparing for trouble. A mild forward or backward weighting can be used in this position, meaning that the weight of the body can be slightly further forward (making the back leg straighter) or a little further back (making the front leg straighter). Many manuscripts show this kind of stance, and in fact some of the manuscripts mentioned above that show a high stance also show a middle stance in other illustrations. This is the style of stance that is seen frequently in the works by Paulus Hector Mair, which is highly relevant because the artwork in Mair's *Opus Amplissimum de Arte Athletica* contains an incredible level of detail.[31]

---

[29] Paulus Kal. *MS 1825*, c.1458-67.
Paulus Kal. *CGM 1507*, c.1470.
Paulus Kal. *MS KK5126*, c.1480.
Hans Talhoffer. *MS Chart.A.558*, 1443.
[30] Emring. *E.1939.65.341.*
[31] Paulus Hector Mair. *MS Dresden C93*, c.1542.

A low stance is one in which the knees are bent as much as possible while still remaining mobile, taking the centre of gravity as low as it can be taken. This stance is almost always accompanied by a forward weight in the fighting manuals that show this kind of stance,[32] although it can also be seen with a backward weight, such as in Meyer's Zornhut. It is in the later manuals from the German longsword system that we see this low type of stance mixed in with the middle type; from this we can surmise either that the later masters chose to adopt a lower stance or that the artists made more of a point to illustrate the depth of the stance. Either way, this is likely a decision made by individuals near the end of the heyday of the longsword, and possibly does not reflect the manner in which the earlier masters would have fought.

What we can take from this overview of the different heights of stances shown in the manuscripts is that there is no single unifying style. Some masters taught low stances, other masters taught a more relaxed stance, some taught stances with a distinct forward weight while others taught stances with a neutral or backward weight, and yet other masters taught a mixture of different types of stances. The lesson here is that a balanced stance, allowing one to move quickly and easily without falling over, is crucial. Sometimes a higher stance will be more appropriate to a situation, and sometimes a very deep stance will be most appropriate. A combatant's stance will likely vary during the course of a fight as different scenarios present themselves.

The advice given to students within the Academy of Historical Arts is to assume a balanced stance that is comfortable and out of which the students can move easily and quickly, and not to worry too much about maintaining a rigid stance for the whole time they fight.

3.1.2 Weighting

Your weight can be held centrally, or it can be forward or backward. The lower the stance, the more extreme this weighting can be without unbalancing the stance. For example, Meyer generally shows low stances and

will often have most of a combatant's weight on the forward leg.[33] In a high stance, such an extreme weighting is impossible.

Forward weighting can allow for explosive forward movement using passing or triangle steps, and helps resist wrestling or push kicks. However, a forward weighting, especially when combined with a low stance, makes backward or side-to-side movement more difficult.

Paulus Hector Mair. *Codex icon.393,* c.1550.

[32] The manuals showing such stances are mainly those by Mair, Meyer and Sutor.

[33] Joachim Meyer. *Gründtliche Beschreibung der Kunst des Fechtens,* 1570.

Backward weighting is the least common weighting. It can be used to take the body further away from the opponent, and so can be helpful when voiding backwards. Backward weighting can also be used for "loading up" or "chambering" a strike, such as in Meyer's Zornhut. By using a backward weighted stance, a combatant can add force to his strike by pushing explosively off the back leg and moving into a forward weighted stance. This is often very telegraphic however, and such a reliance on overpowering strikes may be a sign of a combatant being a Buffel (someone concerned more with power than technical skill).[34]

Backward weighting also makes forward passing and triangle steps more difficult. This is because the more weight there is on a leg, the harder it is to move that leg, but the easier it becomes to push off from that leg in order to move the other leg. Later traditions, such as 17th century rapier, used back-weighted stances more often because they placed a lot of importance on the lunge; however, the German longsword systems do not seem to lunge in the same fashion (because of the different ways in which the weapon is used), so the backwards weighting is less useful here.

A medium weighting is a compromise between these two weightings. It allows the most options in terms of movement. As the weight is equally balanced, it should be equally easy to move forwards, backwards, and side to side. Medium weighting is also less physically strenuous than the other weightings, as weight is distributed evenly between the two legs. If a combatant has weak leg muscles, a medium weighted stance would be recommended over forward or backward weightings.

Eventually, a combatant should reach a level of skill where he can adjust his stance depending on the situation. For example, he may choose to use a deep, forward weighted stance in the Zufechten in order to make large, forward leaps to increase the range of attacks. When in a bind, he may choose to use a more upright, medium weighted stance to offer more options for movement. However, if combatants move forward and wrestling begins, they may then want to use a deeper stance again, in order to provide a stronger grounding so to better prevent being thrown. This is just one example sequence of stance changing, and ultimately what stance one is using at any moment will depend both on circumstance and one's own personal fighting style.

3.1.3 Wage, or Balance/Scale

Many of the 15th and 16th century texts that have been examined during the preparation of this book use the term "wag" or "wage", meaning "balance". This has been the subject of many heated debates in the past, and is

---

[34] Ringeck. *MS Dresden C487* (trans. Keith Farrell, 2011), 31r.

discussed in a famous essay by John Clements.[35] A lot of electronic ink has been spent discussing the issue and debating how it applies to the different medieval and renaissance styles of swordsmanship. The authors of this book believe that while the concept is important, it is merely an issue of common sense, and does not need vast amounts of text to describe it.

In Ringeck's treatise, there is but a single mention of "wage":

> The turner [*verkerer*] subdues,
> runs through and grapples.
> Take the elbow certainly,
> spring against him in the balance [*die wage*].[36]

This appears in one of the original markverse; it is not actually part of Ringeck's gloss at all. Likewise, in the anonymous treatise of the *Goliath* and the *Codex Danzig*, this same piece of markverse is the only mention of "wage" in the whole text.[37]

In the *Codex Wallerstein*, the term "wag" is used much more frequently and seems to refer to a specific deep and balanced stance with both legs somewhat bent as opposed to the "twirch" or "long stance" where the front leg is bent and the back leg is straightened. Contemporary wrestling texts such as that by Fabian von Auerswald appear to refer to a balanced stance in more detail. It makes sense that the *Codex Wallerstein* spends more time talking about "die wag" as a stance than the treatises dealing with longsword fencing, since a lot of the *Codex Wallerstein* material involves grappling or brawling, sometimes with and sometimes without the sword.

To return to the issue of what stance to use when fighting with a longsword, the various sources and treatises in general do not talk about specific stances, and "die wage" seems to be reserved as a stance for when grappling at the sword. The authors of this book teach that as long as a reasonable stance is held, as long as the stance is balanced and the student is not suffering from a lack of balance in a standing position, the stance is acceptable.

3.1.4 Knee Safety

Something that the sources do not describe at all, and that many modern instructors or interpreters fail to teach to students, is positioning of the knee in stance. Too many students will hold a "lazy" stance with the knee collapsed inwards, simply because it is more comfortable and they are concentrating on what they are doing with the sword. It is important that the knees are pushed outwards when in stance and that they are not allowed to turn inwards at all.

---

[35] John Clements. "Scale, Volta and Key." *The ARMA*, 2010.
http://www.thearma.org/VoltaKeyandScale.htm
[36] Ringeck. *MS Dresden C487* (trans. Keith Farrell, 2011), 29v-31r.
[37] Anonymous. *Codex 44.A.8*, 22r.
   Anonymous. *MS Germ.Quart.2020*, c.1510-20, 30r.

Pushing out the knees requires more effort and will tire the legs quickly at first, but letting the knees collapse inwards will result in a weak stance and long-term knee problems. Even a slightly collapsed knee can send students to the physiotherapist for repair after a number of years of only slightly incorrect practice; by simply pushing out the knees when in stance and not letting the knees collapse inwards, the stance will work better and the practitioner will be less likely to suffer debilitating knee pains in the long term.

Although this is not something discussed in the manuals, the authors of this book felt that it would be irresponsible not to add this word of warning based on modern knowledge and practices.

3.2 Footwork

Most German longsword manuals do not talk at any length about footwork, nor do they describe different discrete steps. Rather than specifying various steps that can be taken, the authors have decided to include the elements of footwork that are absolutely essential for the art, and to leave the reader to decide on what exact step to take at any precise moment. Fighting is fluid and unpredictable, hence it is little use telling you which exact steps you must take at all times. You simply take whichever step will keep you safe at any given moment.

Having said that, Liechtenauer's longsword does have some very specific stylistic elements and principles that should be followed.

The first of these is that whenever you strike from your right, you should follow that strike with your right foot. If you strike from the left, you should follow that strike with your left foot.

> If you would show skill,
> go to the left and right with cuts.
> And left with right,
> is how you fight strongly.
>
> This is the longsword's first lesson; that you shall learn to cut properly from both sides, so that you can fight strongly and correctly.
>
> When you want to cut from the right side, stand with your left foot forwards; and when you want to cut from the left side, stand with your right foot forwards.
>
> If you cut with an Oberhaw from the right side, follow after the cut with your right foot. If you do not do this then the cut is poor and insincere, because your right side lingers behind. Then the cut becomes too short and cannot follow the correct arc down towards the other side, in front of the left foot.

Similarly the cut is incorrect if you strike from the left side and do not follow after the cut with the left foot. So mark well, from which side you strike, that the foot follows after the cut. In this manner you can perform all of your techniques correctly and with strength.

And in the same way should all the other cuts be performed.[38]

If you have the left foot forward, you should hold the sword on the right side of your body. When you attack, you must then step forward with your right foot. This ensures your attack has a good range, and ensures that the sword is on the opposite side to your lead leg, which means you will be well balanced.

Note also that this passage says that one should follow the strike with the step. The strike should begin before the step in order to ensure that as you move in towards the opponent, the sword will be covering you and providing some measure of protection.

The other crucial element of footwork in the Liechtenauer tradition is stepping, or leaping, off-line. We are frequently given advice such as:

Take a spring away from the strike with your right foot, far out to his left side.[39]

These off-line leaps can be used with an attack or as part of the defence, since such a movement will help to keep the attacker safe and can create a better line towards targets and openings. Some of the master strikes (the Krumphaw in particular) rely heavily on an off-line leap.

3.3 Gripping the Sword

When you hold the longsword, both hands should normally be holding the grip. Your dominant hand should be the hand closest to the crossguard, so if you are right handed, your right hand should be on top, to help with fine control over the blade. The dominant hand should be right next to the crossguard and as close to the centre of balance on the sword as possible. The further away from the centre of balance you place your dominant hand, the more difficulty you will have controlling the weapon.

The thumb of your dominant hand may wrap around the grip (as if you were holding a hammer) or may rest on the cross or even on the flat of the blade. Ensure that you have a reasonably firm grip of the sword with your dominant hand.

---

[38] Ringeck. *MS Dresden C487* (trans. Keith Farrell, 2011), 11v-13r.
[39] Ibid., 24v-25r.

The non-dominant hand can be placed around the pommel or at the base of the grip next to the pommel. This will at least partially be determined by personal preference and the shape of your pommel: large circular wheel pommels will be uncomfortable to hold in the palm of the hand, whereas "scent stopper", "tear drop" or "fish tail" style pommels will be comfortable to hold in the hand.

The earliest source for the Liechtenauer tradition does actually describe how to hold the sword:

> Also note that a skilled fencer will, before all things, know his sword, and will grip it well with both hands: between the cross guard and the pommel, since this will be a more secure grip than if you held it with one hand on the pommel. Also, you will be able to strike harder and more truly: with the pommel swinging itself, and turning in the strike, you will hit harder than if you held the pommel. When you pull the pommel in the motion of striking, the strike will not be as perfect or as strong. For the sword is like a scale: if the sword is large and heavy, then the pommel must likewise be large and heavy, so that it will balance like a scale.[40]

However, most illustrations in later sources depict fencers holding the sword with the non-dominant hand on or at or around the pommel.[41] So as long as your dominant hand is at the cross, wherever you place your other hand below it will be supported by at least one of the sources.

An exception to this statement is that if the grip of the sword is long enough, the dominant hand may be placed an inch or two back from the crossguard, as can be seen in illustrations throughout the *Goliath*. This has the advantage of providing additional protection to the knuckles of the hand when performing techniques such as the Zwerhaw, but has the disadvantage that the dominant hand is a further inch or two removed from the centre of balance on the sword, making control of the weapon a more difficult task.

It is worth noting that while some translations of the *Hs.3227a* suggest that holding the sword with both hands on the grip is "safer" than having a hand on the pommel, other translations suggest that one grips the sword "more

---

[40] Anonymous. *Hs.3227a*, (trans. Keith Farrell, 2013), 15r.
[41] Such as those found in Talhoffer, in the *Goliath*, in the *Codex Wallerstein*, in the *Glasgow Fechtbüch*, and in Meyer, for example.

surely" when the hand is not on the pommel.[42] The difference in terminology may be small, but in terms of gripping a sword these words can mean quite different things. "More surely" is probably a better translation, since it does make more contextual sense. However, different people have different points of view on this issue.

It is helpful to be able to change how you hold the sword at any moment. Sometimes you should hold the sword tightly; sometimes with a lighter grip, and often you will hold the sword somewhere between these two extremes. Sometimes the hands will rotate around the handle a little in order to make a guard position more comfortable or to put an appropriate amount of leverage into different strikes. As long as you are always in control of the weapon, then it is often helpful to move your hands around the hilt.

The thing to bear in mind is that there is no correct way to hold the sword at all times. You will need to be able to make subtle adjustments in your grip, which unfortunately can only be gained by practice, and is not something we can teach you to do in this guide.

---

[42] David Lindholm, James Wallhausen and Thomas Stoeppler translate the passage with "safer". Grzegorz Żabiński, Jeffrey Hull and Keith Farrell translate the passage with "more surely".

Chapter 4: Guards

4.1 Core Guards of the Liechtenauer Tradition

The guards are the positions one may take with a longsword in the Liechtenauer tradition. Liechtenauer said that there are only four guards worth adopting:

> Four postures alone you will hold, and curse the common. "Ox", "Plough", "Fool", "From the Roof", with these do not be unfamiliar.[43]

However, over the course of the few hundred years during which the Liechtenauer tradition was taught, we see many more guards appear, or the use and position of guards are altered.

One early example is Lang Ort, which the *Hs.3227a* describes briefly as the same position as Vom Tag (i.e. held above the head).[44] Ringeck would later describe Lang Ort as a position with the left leg forward and the tip of the sword pointing at the opponent's chest;[45] the only other time Lang Ort is mentioned in this treatise is where Ringeck describes how to break Lang Ort with the Schilhaw.[46] This suggests that for Ringeck the Lang Ort was simply another position that one might hold, but it does not seem to have been a particularly important one. It is also worth noting that there is nothing in

[43] Ringeck. *MS Dresden C487* (trans. Keith Farrell, 2011), 33v-34r.
[44] Anonymous. *Hs.3227a*, (trans. Keith Farrell, 2013), 32r.
[45] Ringeck. *MS Dresden C487* (trans. Keith Farrell, 2011), 47v & 124r.
[46] Ringeck. *MS Dresden C487* (trans. Keith Farrell, 2011), 32r.

Ringeck's treatise to suggest that strikes or thrusts should end in, or should pass through, Lang Ort.

Much later, Meyer explicitly says to pass through Lang Ort while executing a Schaitelhaw, a Zornhaw, or an Underhaw from Wechselhut.[47] He lists Lang Ort as being a secondary stance, and therefore not as important as the four primary stances, but when using Meyer's striking mechanics one will often pass through Lang Ort in a transitional fashion. In addition, Meyer describes how to use it as a guard proper, and he provides more information than Ringeck about how Lang Ort can be used. So we can see that across the course of the Liechtenauer tradition, the method of using Lang Ort changed dramatically.

Some of these additional guards will be discussed in a later chapter; other guards are so far removed from the Liechtenauer tradition that they have been omitted from this study guide due to time and space constraints.

As we can see, later masters both altered Liechtenauer's art and added to it, so that by the 1600s there were many more guards than when the Liechtenauer tradition first began. This chapter describes the core guards of the tradition, and presents some of the different variants on the core positions.

The authors have chosen to omit illustrations of the different guard positions for a simple reason: there are many different methods to hold each guard as described in the text for each position. Which position would we choose to illustrate, and why? Instead, the descriptions of each position include citations pointing to where the guards are described and/or illustrated in the different manuscripts and primary sources. Readers who would like to see illustrations or images showing these guard positions can follow these citations and look directly at the source material that we have used to form our opinions.

4.1.1 Vom Tag or the Roof Guard:

This is a high guard that will most often be used at a longer distance. It is difficult to thrust or to slice directly from Vom Tag, leaving strikes as the simplest form of attack available from this guard. All of the "Five Strikes" can be performed easily from Vom Tag. There are two standard variants of Vom Tag taught by the Academy of Historical Arts, "shoulder" and "overhead"; these descriptive names are used within the Academy, but are not found in the original sources.

---

[47] Meyer. *Gründtliche Beschreibung der Kunst des Fechtens* (rendered into English by Keith Farrell, 2013, informed by the translations of Rasmusson and Forgeng), 1.9v-1.10r.

4.1.1.1 Shoulder Vom Tag

This guard is shown via illustration in a few of the different sources: the *Codex Danzig*,[48] the *Glasgow Fechtbüch*,[49] the Jörg Breu sketchbook[50] and Mair's great compendium;[51] it is also discussed textually by Ringeck.[52] It is a strong position from which to fight, although it offers less of a protective position than Pflug or Ochs. This guard has the benefit of being very easy to maintain since the sword rests on the shoulder, and can also be a source for many powerful and devastating strikes launched both quickly and comfortably from the shoulder.

To assume this guard on the right side of the body, stand with the left foot forward and rest the short edge of your blade on your right shoulder. The hilt of your weapon should be just in front of your chest, or slightly higher. The blade should always incline back over your shoulder at an angle of between 30º and 60º. The hilt should also not be allowed to drop too low, since dropping the hilt lower than the chest will slow down attacks, as the sword would need to be pushed upwards instead of straight forward when attacking. Your legs should be comfortably spaced at shoulder width apart and with the knees bent, to facilitate a swift and balanced shuffle, step or leap as necessary. Ringeck's description of this guard is simply that you should:

> Stand with the left foot forwards, and hold your sword at your right shoulder.[53]

This guard can also be assumed on the left side of the body by resting the short edge or flat of your blade on your left shoulder and putting your right side forward. There are only a few illustrations that show Vom Tag on the left shoulder, compared to the very large number showing it on the right or above the head. These illustrations can be found in the sketchbook by Jörg Breu[54] and in Paulus Mair's *Opus Amplissimum de Arte Athletica*.[55] This guard could be termed a Mittelhut instead of Vom Tag, since Mair shows it as a position from which to launch a Mittelhaw across the body; however, the illustration does look very similar to Vom Tag on the shoulder, and the text in Mair's *Opus Amplissimum de Arte Athletica* does not identify the guard specifically as a Mittelhut.

---

[48] Anonymous. *Codex 44.A.8*, 2r.

[49] Emring. *E.1939.65.341*, 10r.

[50] Jörg Breu. *Codex I.6.2º.4*, c.1545, 18v – the figure on the right.

[51] Mair. *MS Dresden C93*, 29r & 221v.
   Mair. *Codex icon.393*, 25r & 217v.

[52] Ringeck. *MS Dresden C487*, 34v.

[53] Ringeck. *MS Dresden C487* (trans. Keith Farrell, 2011), 34r.

[54] Breu. *Codex I.6.2º.4*, 18v.

[55] Mair, c.1542. *MS Dresden C93*, 24r & 51r.
   Mair, c.1550. *Codex icon.393*, 20r & 50r.

There is some disagreement within the community about whether or not this position exists in the sources, and Roger Norling has written an article on the subject.[56] The point of view held by the authors of this book is that whether it exists or not in the source material, it is not a particularly important guard position, although it may happen naturally during sparring.

4.1.1.2 Overhead Vom Tag / Oberhut

This variant is universal across most of the masters of the Liechtenauer tradition. We see illustrations of it in manuscripts by many individuals, including: Hans Talhoffer[57] and Paulus Kal,[58] the *Glasgow Fechtbüch*,[59] Christian Egenolph[60] and Hans Medel,[61] Jörg Breu[62] and Paulus Hector Mair,[63] Joachim Meyer[64] and Jakob Sutor.[65] It is also described textually in manuscripts without illustrations, such as those by Jud Lew[66] and Sigmund Ringeck.[67] This guard produces some very powerful Oberhaw strikes, but it is also very open to attack.

To assume this variant, hold the sword directly above your head, with the blade pointing backwards with roughly a 30º to 45º angle. The pommel should just be in your field of view; the left hand on the pommel should be directly in front of your forehead and the right hand should be directly above the crown of your head, effectively creating a right-angled triangle in which the grip of the sword becomes the hypotenuse (the long diagonal). Note that the hands are not pushed far forwards of the head: that variant is shown in a few manuscripts, but it suffers from very vulnerable forearms if the opponent has a fast Zwerhaw. To assume this guard correctly, ensure that your hands are close to your head, better protecting your arms and wrists from incoming strikes. The long edge should face the opponent, and the position of the hands and weapon is the same when either foot is forward.

As a side note, Jakob Sutor calls this position the Oberhut, or "over guard".[68]

---

[56] Roger Norling. "Is there really a Left Vom Tag?" *HROARR*, 2011. http://www.hroarr.com/is-there-really-a-left-vom-tag/

[57] Hans Talhoffer. *Codex icon.394a*, 1467, 2r.

[58] Paulus Kal. *Codex S.554*, c.1506-14, 76r.

[59] Emring. *E.1939.65.341*, 9r & 19v.

[60] Christian Egenolph. *Der Altenn Fechter anfengliche kunst*, 1531, 8v.

[61] Shining. *Codex I.6.2º.5*, 27r.

[62] Breu. *Codex I.6.2º.4*, 18v.

[63] Mair. *MS Dresden C93*, 24r & 25v.
   Mair. *Codex icon.393*, 20r & 21v.

[64] Meyer. *Gründtliche Beschreibung der Kunst des Fechtens*, 1.7r & 1.37r.

[65] Jakob Sutor. *New Kûnstliches Fechtbuch*, 1612, 5.

[66] Anonymous. *Codex I.6.4º.3*, 1450 (trans. Keith Farrell, 2012), 27r.

[67] Anonymous. *Hs.3227a*, (trans. Keith Farrell, 2013), 34v.

[68] Sutor. *New Kûnstliches Fechtbuch*, 5.

4.1.2 Ochs / Oberhangen, or the Ox Guard / Over-hanging

In the *Hs.3227a* the terms Oberhangen and Ochs could be used interchangeably to describe the guard both at rest and in the bind. In the later treatises (such as that by Ringeck), the term Oberhangen was used to refer to an Ochs-like position in a bind.

To assume this guard on the right, put your left foot forward, and hold the back of your right hand above and slightly in front of your right temple, with the point at your opponent's face. The cross-section of the blade can either be perpendicular to the ground, parallel, or any angle in between, but the direction of the blade should be either parallel to the ground or dipped very slightly if the hands are higher than the head.

To assume this guard on the left, put your right foot forward, and hold the palm of your right hand above and slightly in front of your left temple, with the point at the opponent's face. Make sure not to let your hands drop, because if they do, your head will no longer be protected. If you are having problems holding the guard this high for any length of time, place your right thumb on the flat of the blade, this will help until you develop the muscle strength and stamina required to hold the position for an extended length of time.

In terms of the angle at which the cross-section blade should be held with relation to the ground, there are several schools of thought. Illustrations in the sources are not too helpful for this, unfortunately, due to the rules of perspective that illustrators often followed. What is important to note for a modern practitioner is that if the cross section is held parallel to the ground (with horizontal quillons also parallel to the ground) then the knuckles of the hand are exposed in the position. If the long edge of the blade is pointing upwards then the quillon at the long edge helps to protect the knuckles. Because of this, a 45° angle is a reasonably safe way to hold the position and will help to protect your fingers. Each of these three methods can be interpreted from the illustrations, so none of them are definitely wrong; however, the angled method is without doubt the method that is safest for your fingers.

This guard is shown in most of the manuscripts, but the best depictions of the guard can be found in Paulus Mair's *Opus Amplissimum de Arte Athletica*.[69] Illustrations in other manuscripts agree more or less with the above descriptions, but the quality of the artwork is often much inferior to that found in Mair's manuscripts.

---

[69] Mair. *MS Dresden C93*, 24v.
Mair. *Codex icon.393*, 20v.

4.1.3 Pflug / Underhangen or the Plough Guard / Under-hanging

This is a middle guard that can be effectively used in any phase of the fight. Any of the Drei Wunder can be used from Pflug, although the thrust will come most easily and naturally from Pflug. Pflug is also excellent defensively, as it protects most of the torso while keeping the hands low and safe.

When used in the bind, Pflug is referred to as the Underhangen, to contrast it with the other position to which one would commonly wind, the Oberhangen, or Ochs.

4.1.3.1 Middle Pflug

To assume this guard on the right, put your left foot forward and hold your sword by your right hip with the point facing the opponent. The short edge should be on top. To assume this guard on the left, put your right foot forward and hold your sword by your left hip with the point facing the opponent; either edge may be on top.

The distinct advantage of holding Pflug in this manner is that one's hands are safely couched beside the hip and are thus hidden from incoming attacks. Opponents will be unable to strike at one's hands or wrists if the guard is held like this.

This variant of Pflug is shown by a number of different masters, for example Paulus Kal[70] or Andres Paurñfeyndt.[71] It is also described in the *Goliath* manuscript:

> The second guard is called the Plough, and show it like this: stand with the left foot forward and hold your sword with crossed hands with the pommel low and beside your hip at the right side, the short edge above, and the tip pointed at the face.
>
> On the left side show the guard of the Plough like this: stand with the right foot forward and hold your sword near to your hip on the left side, with the long edge above, and the tip pointed at the face. This is the Plough on both sides.[72]

---

[70] Kal. *MS 1825*, 14r.
   Kal. *CGM 1507*, 58r.
   Kal. *Codex S.554*, 15r.
[71] Paurñfeyndt. *Ergrundung Ritterlicher Kunst der Fechterey*, A3v.
[72] Anonymous. *MS Germ.Quart.2020* (trans. Keith Farrell, 2013), 39r.

4.1.3.2 Extended Pflug

This variant is seen in Meyer's treatise,[73] and is also shown by Jörg Wilhalm,[74] Hans Medel[75] and Paulus Hector Mair.[76] To assume this variant, instead of holding the sword at your hip, hold it so that the pommel is on the inside of your lead knee. The hands tend to be held low in this sort of position.

4.1.3.3 Withdrawn Pflug

This variant is seen in the *Codex Danzig*[77] and in the *Goliath*.[78] The depiction of Pflug in these manuscripts has been criticised as being anatomically impossible by some individuals in the HEMA community. The images, particularly in regard to the lead shoulder, may be exaggerated.

To assume this variant, pull back your sword as far as you physically can. You will need to pull your lead arm tight against your body for this to work. There does not seem to be any real benefit when compared to the standard Pflug, and the disadvantages may well outweigh the benefits.

4.1.4 Alber, or the Fool's Guard

This is a low guard is often used defensively, to goad an opponent into attacking one's head by presenting an opening. When the opponent does attack, the fencer in Alber can then counter. Joachim Meyer says this about Alber:

> From this position, one cannot make a finishing strike, until after creating a new opening by way of setting aside an opponent's strike. He is a foolish person if he allows such counter-strike to be made against him.[79]

---

[73] Meyer. *Gründtliche Beschreibung der Kunst des Fechtens,* illustration B.

[74] Jörg Wilhalm Hutter. *Codex I.6.2º.2,* c.1523, 12r-12v.

[75] Shining. *Codex I.6.2º.5,* 29r.

[76] Mair. *MS Dresden C93,* 25r.
   Mair. *Codex icon.393,* 21r.

[77] Anonymous. *Codex 44.A.8,* 1v.

[78] Anonymous. *MS Germ.Quart.2020,* 39v.

[79] Meyer. *Gründtliche Beschreibung der Kunst des Fechtens* (trans. Keith Farrell, 2013), 1.7v.

To assume Alber, point your sword at the ground with the short edge on top, keeping the sword in between you and your opponent. This is the same if either foot is forward. This guard is virtually the same in every manuscript. Sometimes the masters used the guard for unusual purposes, for example Ringeck suggests that:

> If someone cuts against you, do the Krumphaw against him in the manner you have seen before this. Work from Alber, and wind your point against him or cut, thus he must defend himself against you.[80]

Most manuscripts with illustrations show the guard being held in the same manner. These illustrations can be found in the *Glasgow Fechtbüch*[81] and the *Codex Danzig*.[82] Similar images can also be found in the manuscripts created by Paulus Hector Mair,[83] Paulus Kal,[84] Jörg Breu[85] and Jörg Willhalm.[86]

Paulus Kal[87] is an exception to this rule, as he shows a more withdrawn Alber being held. Hans Medel[88] also shows a slightly more withdrawn Alber.

Jakob Sutor[89] shows Alber extended down and forwards in the normal fashion. The interesting point about his illustration, however, is that the leading foot is turned outwards rather than pointing straight forwards. This would facilitate a step forwards and to the right as a following movement.

4.1.5 Early Pflug / Alber

In the *Hs.3227a* the author gives the name Pflug to what is described in later manuscripts as Alber, and likewise gives the name Alber to what is described in later manuscripts as Pflug.[90] This is a point worth knowing, as it can cause some confusion to see a reference to what sounds like a different guard when reading the manuscripts. However, since this nomenclature is in opposition to

---

[80] Ringeck. *MS Dresden C487* (trans. Keith Farrell, 2011), 58v.
[81] Emring. *E.1939.65.341*, 10r.
[82] Anonymous. *Codex 44.A.8*, 2r.
[83] Mair. *MS Dresden C93*, 25v.
    Mair. *Codex icon.393*, 21v.
[84] Kal. *Codex S.554*, 15v.
[85] Breu. *Codex I.6.2º.4*, 16v.
[86] Hutter. *Codex I.6.2º.2*, 14r.
[87] Kal. *MS 1825*, 14v.
    Kal. *CGM 1507*, 58v.
[88] Hans Medel. *Codex I.6.2º.5*, c.1560, 37v.
[89] Sutor. *New Kůnstliches Fechtbuch*, 5.
[90] Anonymous. *Hs.3227a*, 32r.

all of the later treatises in the Liechtenauer tradition, the Academy of Historical Arts does not teach this naming system as standard.

Also, it would appear that this is an error made by the scribe of the *Hs.3227a*, as the scribe also uses the term "zum Pflug Schlagen" (striking to the Pflug) with the same meaning that is described in later manuals (striking to the lower part of the torso).[91] It would be very unlikely that the *Hs.3227a* would talk about striking a Zwerhaw to the shins of an opponent, so we must conclude that the switched names for Pflug and Alber in this manuscript was an error on the part of the scribe.

4.2 Other Variations on the Core Guards

4.2.1 Vom Tag

The manuscripts show a number of different positions for holding the Vom Tag guard. Above the head and by the shoulder are most common, but even so there are still variations between the manuscripts where the illustrations show subtly different positions. The point of view held by the Academy of Historical Arts is that any and all of these positions are valid; indeed, Academy instructors often move subtly between these variations as each position has minor differences in performance.

These are the variations of the Vom Tag guard that the authors have found by searching through several treatises. Other HEMA groups and instructors might hold the guard in a different fashion, but as far as the authors are concerned, these variations listed here are the only variations with historical provenance. Distinction has been made between them in this text solely for the purpose of sourcing the techniques and guards found in this discipline.

4.2.1.1 Vom Tag with Resting Flat

This variant is described in the *Codex Lew*,[92] the *Codex Speyer*[93] and the *Opus Amplissimum de Arte Athletica*.[94] The interesting detail for this variant is that the text specifies that the flat of the blade should rest on the shoulder:

> So mark when you come near to him, set the left foot forwards and hold your sword with the flat on your right shoulder.[95]

---

[91] Ibid., 27r & 28r.
[92] Anonymous. *Codex I.6.4º.3*, c.1450, 16v-17r.
[93] Anonymous. *MS M.I.29*, 1491, 21r.
[94] Mair. *MS Dresden C93*, 91v.
  Mair. *Cod.Vindob.10825*, 77r.
[95] Anonymous. *Codex I.6.4º.3* (trans. Keith Farrell, 2013), 16v-17r.

It is worth noting, however, that Vom Tag is only described like this in the section about the Zwerhaw, whereas in other parts of the manuscript Vom Tag is described as being held above the head. This may mean that this variation on Vom Tag is associated specifically with performing the Zwerhaw; but the position can also be used as an origin for other strikes.

The benefit of this variant is that it is very energy efficient and easy to maintain. It can also be easier to move from this position to a strike such as the Zwerhaw or Schilhaw, as thumbing the blade is easier from this resting position than from the position with the short edge resting on the shoulder.

4.2.1.2 High Vertical Vom Tag

Two of the manuscripts by Paulus Kal show an interesting version of Vom Tag where the right foot is forwards and the sword is held almost vertically, slightly in front of and to the side of the head. In one of the illustrations, the fencer is left-handed[96] and so the right foot forward stance is not unusual; the other illustration shows a right-handed fencer[97] with a right leg forward stance, which is peculiar.

Pains should be taken, however, to distinguish between the right foot forward Vom Tag position held by the right-handed fencer in this illustration and the right foot forward Vom Tag position held by a lot of modern longsword practitioners: the modern position of the sword resting on the shoulder, or at least with the hands low, is not what is shown in the illustration. The illustration shows the hands above the head, with the sword held almost vertically up into the air, so this illustration cannot be used to support the modern right leg forward Vom Tag position.

4.2.1.3 Vom Tag Above the Shoulder

There has been much debate in the HEMA community over the years about whether a shoulder Vom Tag should rest on the shoulder or should be held a few inches above the shoulder. Unfortunately the manuscripts do not give a clear and definite answer to this question; the illustrations can support either point of view, the textual descriptions are vague because the German word *an* can mean "at" or "by", but can also mean "on".[98] Since the language is ambiguous, and the illustrations can be ambiguous, it is impossible to say if either point of view is entirely right or entirely wrong. While the Academy of Historical Arts prefers to teach the shoulder Vom Tag as resting on the shoulder, it is perfectly reasonable to hold the weapon in the same fashion as normal but a few inches above shoulder instead of at rest.

---

[96] Kal. *CGM 1507*, 58v.

[97] Kal. *MS 1825*, 18v.

[98] In 2012, Matt Clarke posted something the notion to the HEMA Alliance forum here: http://hemaalliance.com/discussion/viewtopic.php?f=20&t=2394

A little later in the same month, Andreas Engström wrote an excellent description of this problem in a different thread:

http://hemaalliance.com/discussion/viewtopic.php?f=3&t=2459&p=34117#p34117

4.2.1.4 Forward High Vom Tag

This guard is similar to the overhead Vom Tag, but instead of holding the hilt of the sword close to and above the head, the hilt is pushed further forwards so that the arms are almost outstretched. This guard is seen in some of Paulus Mair's illustrations.[99] This position might be a little more imposing in terms of presenting the sword closer to an opponent's face, and may well be a position taken by inexperienced fighters, but it has two main drawbacks: strikes from this position lack the power and reach of the overhead Vom Tag, and the forearms and hands are very open and exposed to attacks by an opponent.

4.2.1.5 Right Leg Forward, Sword on Right Shoulder

This variation is seen regularly in modern sparring but has no basis in the historical manuals. The most similar illustration to justify the position can be found in a manuscript by Paulus Kal,[100] but as described above in the section for the "high vertical Vom Tag", the illustration does not actually support the modern variation that appears commonly in sparring.

Fighting with the right leg forward and holding the sword on the right shoulder reduces the amount of distance that can be covered with a strike reduced quite dramatically. If both combatants are at a distance where this sort of guard is effective, then quite simply both combatants have made a mistake in terms of judging distance and range. At this distance, the fight boils down to who can twitch, re-act and strike the fastest.

If you find yourself assuming this sort of position then something has gone wrong with your approach to the fight. You should discipline yourself to step back and assume a proper guard position again, so that you can spar with correct techniques at the correct sort of distance. This disciplined approach to sparring may result in fewer victories in the short term, but in the long term it will help you to learn more about the art of fencing and in particular to learn how to apply correct techniques with the correct range to cover the distance that presents itself in sparring.

4.2.2 Zornhut, or the Wrath Guard

To adopt Zornhut, assume a shoulder Vom Tag, shift into a back-weighted stance and rotate the sword so that it hangs down your back. You may even point the sword at your opponent if you are twisted far enough.

This stance can generate a more powerful Zornhaw than Vom Tag. However, it can be also very telegraphic, unless the striking mechanics are smooth and subtle. If not used properly, this guard can be indicative of a Buffel, or

---

[99] Mair. *Codex icon.393*, 51r & 53r.
[100] Kal. *MS 1825*, 18v.

"Buffalo"; someone who uses strength without due regard for technique and skill.[101] Jörg Wilhalm shows the Zornhut on the left shoulder,[102] presumably so that the resulting Oberhaw can generate as much force as a more natural Zornhaw from Vom Tag on the right shoulder.

Later in the tradition, Joachim Meyer makes extensive use of the Zornhut, and says that it can be held on both the left and right shoulders.[103]

4.2.3 Hangennort, or Hanging Point

The Hangennort is similar to Ochs, except that the point is dropped more so that it hangs down towards the ground. The blade is angled in such a fashion that it covers the body against an incoming attack. For example, if an opponent struck an Oberhaw from his right shoulder, then the defender's Hangennort would be like a right Ochs but more angled down and to the left so that the body would be hidden behind the blade. If an opponent struck a long edge Zwerhaw from his left then the defender's Hangennort would be like a left Ochs, angled down and to the right so that the body again could be hidden behind the blade. This is an excellent guard for covering a large amount of one's body, and it is a good starting point for a number of counter attacks.

Interestingly, this guard is only seen in much later manuscripts. The earlier manuscripts talk about the Vier Hengen (the four hangings), and these will be discussed in the chapter on Binding and Winding. We see reference to the Hangennort by Paulus Hector Mair,[104] Joachim Meyer[105] and Jakob Sutor.[106]

4.2.4 Einhorn, or Unicorn

The Einhorn, or Unicorn, is a version of the Ochs guard. To perform this guard, hold an Ochs guard with the hands slightly higher than normal and with the tip of the blade pointing up at an angle, instead of holding the blade horizontally or with a slight dip as with the normal Ochs. This guard is shown by Wilhalm[107] and Meyer,[108] and is described in the following fashion:

> In the Zufechten, come forward with your left foot, and do the Winging strike on both sides, as if you intended to stand in the Key. Go up with your hands crossed, above your head to the right, so that the tip goes high to the outside. This is called the Unicorn, and you will stand as shown by the rightmost figure in illustration E.[109]

---

[101] Ringeck. *MS Dresden C487* (trans. Keith Farrell, 2011), 31r.

[102] Hutter. *Codex I.6.2º.2*, 6v.

[103] Meyer. *Gründtliche Beschreibung der Kunst des Fechtens*, 1.7v & 1.35v.

[104] Mair. *MS Dresden C93*, ff. 27v, 43r & 43v.
 Mair. *Codex icon.393*, ff. 23v, 39r & 39v.

[105] Meyer. *Gründtliche Beschreibung der Kunst des Fechtens*, 9r.

[106] Sutor. *New Künstliches Fechtbuch*, 6.

[107] Hutter. *Codex I.6.2º.2*, 13v.

[108] Meyer. *Gründtliche Beschreibung der Kunst des Fechtens*, ff. 1.9r, 1.37v & 1.54r.

[109] Ibid. (trans. Keith Farrell, 2013), 1.9r-1.9v.

Paulus Hector Mair's treatises illustrate this guard and even describe it,[110] but it is not given a specific name in his works. Although Mair's illustrations are rather different from the images in the texts by Meyer and Wilhalm, his description is similar to Meyer's:

> Stand with your left foot forwards and with crossed hands (with the left hand over your right arm) hold the short edge towards the man.[111]

However, this description and illustration of the guard comes in the page entitled "Two windings-in with the sword" so it would appear that guard is not the principal focus of the text, but rather a step towards achieving the techniques of winding in at an opponent.

4.2.5 Schlussel, or the Key

> Stand with your left foot forward, hold the sword with the hilt and crossed hands in front of your chest, so that the short edge rests on your left arm and the tip is pointed at your opponent's face.[112]

Schlussel is similar to the Ochs, except instead of holding the sword at or above the head, the short edge of the sword should rest on the left arm and should be held no higher than the shoulder. The Schlussel is a guard that appears very late within the Liechtenauer tradition, and at first seems not to be much more than than a weaker variant of Ochs. Meyer admits that the Schlussel appears to be weak, but despite this, he asserts that in fact it can counter any other guard.

> This guard is called the Key, since from this position all other techniques and positions can be defeated. Although this holds true for other positions, they require more force to do so than this one. In the same way as a key, a small instrument, can open a strong lock without much trouble or force, this 'weak' position can counter all other techniques and positions with art and skill, without much trouble or force.[113]

4.3 Other Non-Core Guards

4.3.1 The Lower Guards

There are other low guards that are mentioned in the assorted fechtbücher, although we often lack enough description in any one manual to be able to say for certain how each fencing master intended the guards to be held. The best we can do is to compare a number of sources and take a rough average of how the guards are described, and to bear in mind that each master had a slightly different interpretation, so it is alright and indeed reasonable to form our own educated interpretations of how each guard can be held.

---

[110] Mair. *MS Dresden C93*, 45r.
   Mair. *Codex icon.393*, 41r.
[111] Ibid. (trans. Keith Farrell, 2013), 45r.
[112] Meyer. *Gründtliche Beschreibung der Kunst des Fechtens* (trans. Keith Farrell, 2013), 1.9r.
[113] Ibid., 1.38v.

44

It is also worth noting that when talking about the Pflug the *Hs.3227a* tells us that:

> After a displacement, it is called either the Barrier Guard or just the Gate.[114]

However, the *Hs.3227a* also discusses the use of the Eysenen Pfort, where we are told that when facing multiple opponents you should:

> Then place forward either foot, and with the Gate you will create a shield by the placement of the point towards the ground.[115]

This quote suggests that you can hold the Eysenen Pfort without displacing anything. Bearing in mind the Pflug/Alber discrepancy discussed earlier in this chapter, these two quotes tell us that the author of the *Hs.3227a* considered the Schrankhut and the Eysenen Pfort as being variants, or possibly applications, of Alber. It may therefore be possible to conclude that any low guard can be considered as a variant of Alber.

In the *Codex Speyer*, we can find similar evidence that low guards sometimes had more than one name, in the section that compares the longsword positions to those used when fighting with a messer (a long knife).[116] The scribe notes that Alber is also named "ysen pfortt" and that it is just a single position. So even though some masters differentiated between Alber and this guard, others apparently did not.

For the sake of convenience and clarity, when we use the term Alber in this book, we are referring to the more standard version as described earlier in this chapter, rather than to any other low guard.

4.3.1.1 Eysenen Pfort, or Iron Gate

This guard is very similar to Alber, except that it is held to the side instead of to the front. This makes it less tiring to hold, and opens the possibility for short edge strikes or defensive sweeps. We see the guard shown and named "eisnin portt" by Jörg Wilhalm[117] and "yszni port" by Hans Talhoffer.[118]

Ringeck suggests that sweeps should be performed from "Nebenhut out to your left side",[119] but the guard described is more like the Iron Gate. However, in his gloss in the *Glasgow Fechtbüch*, he writes that the sweeps should be performed from "eysenen pfort" out to the left side.[120] Given that other masters have named this guard the Iron Gate (albeit with a myriad of

---

[114] Anonymous. *Hs.3227a* (trans. Keith Farrell, 2013), 32r.
[115] Ibid., 44v.
[116] Magister Andreas. *MS M.I.29*, 1491, 6v.
[117] Hutter. *Codex I.6.2º.2*, 14v.
[118] Talhoffer. *Codex icon.394a*, 9v.
[119] Ringeck. *MS Dresden C487* (trans. Keith Farrell, 2011), 49r.
[120] Emring. *E.1939.65.341*, 22v.

different spellings, often with different spellings even in the same paragraph of the same manuscript), it makes sense that the term in the *Glasgow Fechtbüch* is correct, and that the term in the *Codex Ringeck* is erroneous – or that Ringeck (or one of the people reproducing his gloss) changed his terminology at some point. The second explanation makes the most sense.

The *Hs.3227a* spends quite a lot of ink describing the "eyserynen pforten" guard, and although it never appears in Liechtenauer's markverse, the scribe states that the stance is one of the most useful guards used by Liechtenauer himself: "Here rightly begins the very best fencing by the aforesaid master", which can only suggest that Liechtenauer recognised the guard as very useful. The full description reads as follows:

> Here begins the very best of fencing known to the aforementioned master. I tell you that it is called the Iron Gate, which you will understand soon. If four or six peasants attack you, then place forward either foot, and with the Gate you will create a shield by the placement of the point towards the ground. Note how this should be done: position yourself so that they are all in front of you, and so that no one can sneak behind you. Now note what you should do: when they attack you with strike or thrust, go up from the ground and set them aside. Thus you shame them![121]

Meyer describes his version of "Eisenport", which bears no resemblance to any other version of this guard by any other master:

> Stand with your right foot forward and hold your sword with the hilt in front of the knee, with straight and outstretched arms, and angle your point up towards your opponent's face. So the sword is in front of you, giving protection, like an iron gate. When you stand with your feet wide and with your body low, you can set aside all cuts and thrusts from this position.[122]

This is clearly a variation on Pflug, and Meyer admits that it is used more for rapier than for longsword.[123]

4.3.1.2 Nebenhut, or Near Guard

The Nebenhut is held down beside the legs, pointing (more or less) to the rear. Meyer describes the Nebenhut like so:

> Stand with your left foot forward. Hold your sword at your right side with the point towards the ground, with the pommel above, and with the short edge towards you.[124]

This guard is not pictured very often in the manuscripts; in fact, Talhoffer[125] shows a single picture of the guard, and Falkner[126] shows the reverse of Talhoffer's image. The *Codex Wallerstein*[127] also shows a single uncaptioned

---

[121] Anonymous. *Hs.3227a* (trans. Keith Farrell, 2013), 44v.
[122] Meyer. *Gründtliche Beschreibung der Kunst des Fechtens* (trans. Keith Farrell, 2013), 1.8r.
[123] Ibid.
[124] Ibid.
[125] Talhoffer. *Codex icon.394a*, 14r.
[126] Peter Falkner. *MS KK5012*, c.1495, 12r.
[127] Anonymous. *Codex I.6.4º.2*, c.1470, 76r.

picture of this position, while Mair[128] depicts the guard as the beginning and end points of the Wechselhaw but without naming the guard itself.

Ringeck describes the Nebenhut as being held out to the side, but he may have been using this name as a catch-all term for lower guards.[129]

4.3.1.3 Schrankhut, or Barrier Guard

The Schrankhut is a vertical low guard, with the point close to the floor and the crossguard held at chest height. Schrankhut fulfills much the same role as Alber, in that the sword is held low to goad an opponent in to attack. It is often used as the starting point for the Krumphaw, and can also be the middle point for a Krumphaw launched from the right shoulder.

Ringeck's treatise includes a concise description of the Schrankhut:

> When you fence with someone and come close to him, stand with the left foot forwards and put your sword with the point towards the ground on your right side, so that the long edge is upwards; and from the left side the short edge downwards and the right foot forwards.[130]

The guard is mentioned in the *Hs.3227a*,[131] which shows that it is not a late addition to the discipline. However, it is not one of Liechtenauer's core guards, as it does not feature in any of the markverse. We see it illustrated in manuscripts by Andre Paurñfeyndt[132] and Paulus Mair,[133] in the *Goliath*,[134] and by Joachim Meyer[135] and Jakob Sutor.[136]

---

[128] Mair. *MS Dresden C93*, 54r.
  Mair. *Codex icon.393*, 50r.
[129] Ringeck. *MS Dresden C487*, 49r.
[130] Ibid. (trans. Keith Farrel, 2011), 24r.
[131] Anonymous. *Hs.3227a*, 48v.
[132] Paurñfeyndt. *Ergrundung Ritterlicher Kunst der Fechterey*, A4v & B2v.
[133] Mair. *MS Dresden C93*, 53v.
  Mair. *Codex icon.393*, 49v.
[134] Anonymous. *MS Germ.Quart.2020*, 19v.
[135] Meyer. *Gründtliche Beschreibung der Kunst des Fechtens*, illustration F.
[136] Sutor. *New Kûnstliches Fechtbuch*, 6.

4.3.1.4 Wechselhut, or Change Guard

The Wechselhut (sometimes just called the Wechsel) is held down low, with the point forward and to the side. It is the natural end position for an Oberhaw that cuts down and finishes by pointing to the ground. This means that the angle is somewhere between that of Alber and that of Eysenen Pfort, although this is not set in stone. The best way to think about this guard is that it is a comfortable location in which to end an Oberhaw and from which to launch an Underhaw back up along the same line, making it the natural middle point for the Wechselhaw. Meyer describes it as follows:

> Stand with your right foot forward and hold your weapon with the point (or weak) towards the ground at your side, with the short edge facing your opponent, as is shown by the figure in illustration D.[137]

We see the Wechselhut illustrated and named in manuscripts by Talhoffer,[138] Meyer[139] and Sutor.[140]

In Mair[141] we see a guard named as the beginning and end points of the Wechselhaw, but it is depicted as being held behind the body in a position similar to the Nebenhut mentioned above. In the Codex Wallerstein[142] we see the same image, without any captions at all. Since Mair does not give a name for the guard position, we must infer that the Wechselhaw can come from whatever low guard is most comfortable and appropriate at the time. This is quite a reasonable assumption to make, and allows for plenty of options during the randomness of combat.

Mair makes a second illustration of "the Wechsel" where the sword is held pointed down to the side and forwards,[143] almost in between the Eysenen Pfort and Alber. This is quite a comfortable position in which to end an Oberhaw, and a comfortable position from which to commence an Underhaw back up to one of the higher guards.

4.3.1.5 An Unnamed Low Guard

Another interesting illustration is seen in Mair [144] and the *Codex Wallerstein*.[145] The combatant on the left holds a guard very similar to the Wechselhut as described and shown by Talhoffer, Meyer and Sutor. Again the *Codex Wallerstein* provides no captions, but Mair entitles the illustration "A

---

[137] Meyer. *Gründtliche Beschreibung der Kunst des Fechtens* (trans. Keith Farrell, 2013), 1.8r.
[138] Talhoffer. *Codex icon.394a*, 2v.
[139] Meyer. *Gründtliche Beschreibung der Kunst des Fechtens,* illustration D.
[140] Sutor. *New Kůnstliches Fechtbuch*, 9.
[141] Mair. *MS Dresden C93*, 54r.
   Mair. *Codex icon.393*, 50r.
[142] Anonymous. *Codex I.6.4º.2*, 76r.
[143] Mair. *MS Dresden C93*, 56r.
   Mair. *Codex icon.393*, 52r.
[144] Mair. *MS Dresden C93*, 58r.
   Mair. *Codex icon.393*, 54r.
[145] Anonymous. *Codex I.6.4º.2*, 77r.

guard from the Plough against the Oberhaw",[146] and displays a low guard with characteristics similar to the three guards described above, particularly the Wechselhut. However, this guard is not given a name, and the position is used for tempting an opponent to strike at the head from a high guard, so that one can move from this low couched position to deliver a powerful counter strike. The term Wechsel is not used at all in Mair's caption for this position or its subsequent plays, so we must assume that the guard is different from the Wechselhut and is not used as part of the Wechselhaw.

4.3.1.6 Helpful Visualisations

Since many of the masters describe the low guards in varying fashions, and illustrations depict the guards being held at slightly different angles, it might be helpful to visualise a very rough rule of thumb:

- if the sword is in the 90º arc in front of the body, then it is roughly Alber;
- if the sword rests in the 90º arc to the left or right, then it is roughly Eysenen Pfort;
- if the sword is in the 90º arc to the left or right, ready to strike, then it is roughly Wechsel;
- if the sword is in the 90º arc behind the body, then it is roughly Nebenhut;
- if the tip is to the ground and the blade is almost vertical, then it is roughly Schrankhut.

This means it does not matter precisely where the guard is held, as there is likely a text or illustration that describes the rough position, using roughly those terms for the guards. At the very least, the intentions behind the guards work with this general rule: Ringeck's sweeps will work from anywhere in the 90º side arc; Meyer's Krumphaw from the Nebenhut will work from anywhere in the 90º back arc, the Wechselhaw will work from anywhere in the 90º side arc, the Kron defence from Alber will work from anywhere in the 90º front arc. This keeps the issue of low guards nice and simple, and helps to remove much of the confusion during practice and/or sparring.

4.3.2 Reversed Hand Ochs

Sometimes the manuscripts show figures holding an Ochs with the left hand in a different position. There are some subtle differences in this variation of the normal Ochs guard, and these are outlined below.

4.3.2.1 Reversed Hand Ochs, from *Codex Wallerstein*

To assume the left side variant, hold the sword in a left Ochs and let go with the left hand. Bring the left hand behind the sword, and then hold the sword so that both your palms are facing in towards yourself. This guard is also depicted with the left leg forward, rather than with the right leg forward, as is more commonly seen with a left Ochs. This is seen in the *Codex*

---

[146] Mair. *MS Dresden C93* (trans. Keith Farrell, 2013), 58r.

Wallerstein.[147] When you meet with an opponent and he is hard in the bind, instead of winding into a more conventional Ochs, you could also move into this Reversed Ochs sort of position.

To assume the right side variant, hold the sword in a right Ochs and let go with the left hand. Bring the left arm over the right (so that it is now the closest arm to your face) and grab onto the handle with the left palm facing the same direction as the right palm. This is seen in the *Codex Wallerstein.*[148]

Dierk Hagedorn and Christian Tobler presented a pair of videos to discuss these positions during an experimental workshop in 2010 that explored these reversed-hand grips.[149]

4.3.2.2 Reversed Hand Ochs, according to Mair

This is virtually the same as the *Codex Wallerstein* variant, and is seen in Mair's manuscripts.[150] The key difference between Mair's reversed hand Ochs and the *Codex Wallerstein* reversed hand Ochs is that in the *Codex Wallerstein*, the individual goes into a powerful and defensive bind using this position, that then becomes offensive. Mair instead goes into an offensive reversed hand Ochs with the intent to stab his opponent or with the intent to slice his opponent's arms with the upward motion, since his opponent is standing in Vom Tag with the forearms dangerously forward and exposed.

4.3.2.3 Reversed Hand Ochs, according to Falkner

This position is illustrated in the manuscript of Peter Falkner.[151] To assume this variant, hold the sword in a right Ochs, and switch the left grip so the left palm is facing the same direction as the right palm. The right wrist should still cross over the left in this variant, as in a standard Ochs; notice how this point distinguishes Falkner's version of this guard from the version in the *Codex Wallerstein.*

Falko Fritz and Christian Tobler presented a video to discuss this position during an experimental workshop in 2010 that explored these reversed-hand grips.[152]

---

[147] Anonymous. *Codex I.6.4º.2*, 3v.

[148] Ibid., 77r.

[149] Dierk Hagedorn and Christian Tobler. 2010. *"The Reversed Hand in the Codex Wallerstein (1/2)"*: http://www.youtube.com/watch?v=QOamzdO-th0

Dierk Hagedorn and Christian Tobler. 2010. *"The Reversed Hand in the Codex Wallerstein (2/2)"*: http://www.youtube.com/watch?v=odAleRpD5hY

[150] Mair. *MS Dresden C93*, 56v.

Mair, c.1550. *Codex icon.393*, 52v.

[151] Falkner. *MS KK5012*, 12v.

[152] Falko Fritz and Christian Tobler. 2010. *"The Reversed Hand in Peter Falkner (KK 5012)"*: http://www.youtube.com/watch?v=94p1R6RZ5Oo

4.3.3 Kron, or Crown

The Kron is a guard that is mentioned in almost every treatise, but usually only in the context of the Schaitelhaw. This position is defeated always by the Schaitelhaw sequence.

Some illustrations show the guard held with the blade held vertically (or at a slight angle) with the hands up and in front of the head.[153] Other illustrations show the Kron as a halfsword position,[154] and Wilhalm writes that the Kron was done with the sword in the "armoured hand",[155] a convention that indicated a halfsword grip.

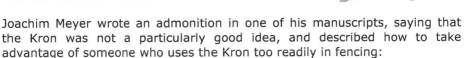

The Zettel suggests that the position might be useful: "That which comes from him, the Crown takes away."[156] However, it appears only to be a middle-step in the process of using the Schaitelhaw to defeat Alber: if the defender leaves Alber and assumes Kron, then the Kron might well catch the Schaitelhaw, but then the attacker will disengage from the Kron and will slice the defender's forearms.

Joachim Meyer wrote an admonition in one of his manuscripts, saying that the Kron was not a particularly good idea, and described how to take advantage of someone who uses the Kron too readily in fencing:

> Do not rely on the Crown,
> it will bring you shame and injury.
>
> Note: when you go up with the crossguard in a horizontal fashion, to displace a strike, this is called the Crown. If you notice that he wants to use the Crown to displace your Oberhaw, do not let your Oberhaw land, but instead tug the strike away. Thus his movement is wasted, and you may cut a Mittelhaw with the long edge across his forearm or wrist.
>
> In a similar fashion, if you notice that someone often goes up high with the displacement, then act as if you would cut high at him. Do not land the cut, but instead come round with the Zwirch with flat or long edge to his lower openings, or strike at his ears behind his arms.[157]

This admonition fits with the information and sequences in the earlier sources as well, although the earlier sources do not say explicitly that Kron is bad.

---

[153] Emring. *E.1939.65.341*, 7v & 9r.

[154] Hutter, c.1523. *CGM 1711*, 41r-42r.

[155] Ibid. (trans. Alex Bourdas, 2012), 41r.

[156] Ringeck. *MS Dresden C487* (trans. Keith Farrell, 2011), 33r.

[157] Joachim Meyer. *MS A.4º.2*, 1560 (rendered into English by Keith Farrell, 2013, informed by the translation by Kevin Maurer), 37r-37v.

4.3.4 Brechfenster, or Window Breaker

The Brechfenster appears to be virtually the same as the Kron guard, just a different name used by different masters.[158] Kron seems to be a name used more by the earlier authors and Brechfenster seems to be a much later term.

---

[158] Mair. *MS Dresden C93*, 44r.
   Mair. *Codex icon.393*, 40r.

Chapter 5: Strikes

5.1 Concepts for Attacking

5.1.1 Blossen

There are four main targets at which one should strike on an unarmoured opponent. Imagine the outline of a torso, divide it in half with a vertical line running down the centre of the head and body, and then divide it into quarters with a horizontal line running across the torso at roughly rib height. These four quarters (upper left, upper right, lower left, lower right) are known as the four "Blossen" or four openings. The two upper openings include the head, shoulders and chest; the two lower openings include the stomach and guts, the groin and the thighs.

Ringeck describes the four openings as follows:

> Here you will learn about people's four openings, against which you will always fence. The first opening is on the right sight, the second on the left side, above the man's belt. The other two are likewise on the right and left sides under the belt. Always pay attention to the openings in Zufechten. His openings you shall skillfully seek without danger: with thrusts with the outstretched point, with travelling after and with all other techniques.[159]

---

[159] Ringeck. *MS Dresden C487* (trans. Keith Farrell, 2011), 22v-23r.

5.1.2 Zum Ochs Schlagen / Zum Pflug Schlagen

"Zum Ochs Schlagen" simply means striking to the upper openings, so aiming one's strikes at the head, neck or shoulders. "Zum Pflug Schlagen" means striking to the lower openings, so aiming one's strikes at the ribs, lower torso and under-arms. One should not concentrate on attacking a single opening, but rather should chain together attacks towards different openings into a single flurry; this concept is important when attacking an opponent, and the German masters belabour this point. For example:

> How one should fight against the four openings with the Zwerhaw. Do the Zwerhaw to the lower openings [*Zum Pflug*], and strike fiercely to the higher openings [*Zum Ochs*]. This is how you will cut against the four openings with the Zwerhaw when you stand against someone. When you come against him in the beginning [*Zufechten*]; when the time is correct for you, run towards him and cut with the Zwerhaw against the lower opening on his left side. This is called "to strike against the plough" [*Zum Pflug Schlagen*].[160]

5.1.3 Vorschlag

The Vorschlag (the "before strike") is the first strike in an armed exchange. The combatant who controls the Vor (the "before") is the person who throws the Vorschlag.

The *Hs.3227a* suggests that the combatant who makes the Vorschlag has an advantage in the fight. Many sections in the treatise talk about "gaining" the Vorschlag, and insist that this is something that combatants should try to do. For example, it is stated that:

> In all fencing, someone may defeat a Master with his strike if only he is bold and makes the first strike.[161]

However, the Vorschlag should not be used by itself in isolation. It is merely the first in a series of quickly flowing techniques with the intention of taking the initiative and forcing the opponent to be on the defensive. The *Hs.3227a* gives this further advice:

> Once the opponent makes his defence against your first strike, make more attacks swiftly against his other openings, with a variety of techniques.[162]

5.1.4 Nachschlag

A Nachschlag is an "after-strike" in an armed exchange. Once the Vorschlag has been thrown by one of the combatants, any following attacks thrown are termed to be Nachschlag. If a combatant has won the Vorschlag then it is important to follow up with a Nachschlag, for the following reason:

---

[160] Ibid., 28v-29r.
[161] Anonymous. *Hs.3227a* (trans. Keith Farrell, 2013), 20v.
[162] Ibid.

Then, before the opponent can recover himself and make an action, you should make your after strike, and so he will have to defend again and will not be able to make his own attacks. So when you throw your first strike, if the opponent defends himself against this, you will always be able to make the after strike while he is still occupied with parrying.[163]

In fact, it is so important to keep pressing the advantage of having won the first strike that one should make a flurry of attacks and not worry about landing every strike. Of course, the more strikes that land, the better, but the *Hs.3227a* suggests that the flurry of Nachschlag is more important than ensuring that the Vorschlag lands on target:

> When you throw the first strike, no matter if you hit or miss, you should immediately make the after strike before he has the same opportunity. So when you want to throw the first strike, you must also make the after strike with speed, so that he cannot make his own strikes at you.[164]

5.1.5 Überlauffen

Überlauffen, overrunning or reaching-over, is one of the principles of Liechtenauer's art, and it states that high attacks (these can be strikes, thrusts, or slices) are better than low attacks (although there is a caveat to this as will be shown below). By countering a low attack with a high response, the attacker can be beaten. This is simply because a high attack has greater reach than low attack.

> In Zufechten, when he aims for a lower opening with a cut or a thrust, do not defend yourself against it. Rather, wait until you can reach over him with a strike from above against the head or a thrust from above, so he will be defeated by you, because all Oberhaw and all high attacks reach further than lower strikes.[165]

This is a simple geometric issue, illustrated by the following diagram. Imagine that point A is the position of the swordsman's shoulders, and points B and C represent possible endpoints of an attack. Lines AB and AC are the same length, but because AC is pointing downwards, it has less horizontal "reach" than AB. The grey dotted lines show the space and reach that is lost by attacking along line AC.

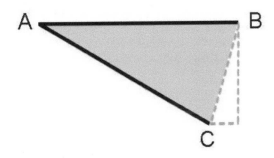

163 Ibid., 21r.
164 Ibid., 38r.
165 Ringeck. *MS Dresden C487* (trans. Keith Farrell, 2011), 39v.

This diagram shows that attacks to the upper openings will have more reach than attacks to the lower openings. This means that when an opponent attacks to your legs, then instead of blocking or parrying, the response should be simply to attack to his upper openings. This may need to be accompanied by a step backward, to ensure safety for your legs, but the higher attack should reach over the lower attack and land the strike while the lower attack is out of range.

It was mentioned above that there is a caveat to the principle of Überlauffen. At engaging distance, this is an important concept, but it does not apply in Krieg:

> When the war goes high, he will be shamed below.[166]

About the winding plays associated with the Zornhaw, Ringeck wrote:

> In this way he will be cut down in the Krieg both above and below, because you (unlike he) can perform the movements correctly.[167]

Therefore during Krieg one can strike, thrust or slice to both high and low targets, and if the opponent is skilled, so can he. In short, Überlauffen does not apply during Krieg because of the closer distance at which Krieg must be performed.

5.2 Basic Strikes of the Liechtenauer Tradition

> This is the longsword's first lesson; that you shall learn to cut properly from both sides.[168]

5.2.1 Oberhaw

An Oberhaw is literally an "over-strike", an attack striking down onto the opponent's body, describing a downward arc. The most obvious Oberhaw is a downwards cut with the long edge, coming from one of the Vom Tag positions. An example of such an Oberhaw is the Zornhaw. However, an Oberhaw can also be made with the short edge: the Schilhaw is an example of a short edge Oberhaw. The simplest way to think of this kind of attack is that an Oberhaw is any strike that comes from a higher position and strikes down onto the opponent.

---

[166] Anonymous. *Hs.3227a* (trans. Keith Farrell, 2013), 23r.
[167] Ringeck. *MS Dresden C487* (trans. Keith Farrell, 2011), 21v-22r.
[168] Ibid., 11v-12r.

5.2.2 Underhaw

An Underhaw is literally an "under-strike", an attack striking up into the opponent's body, describing an upward arc. The *Hs.3227a* states that all other strikes come from the Oberhaw and Underhaw, making these very important techniques to practice and with which to become both familiar and comfortable:

> Know that all possible strikes come from only two strikes: the strikes from above and from below, from both sides. These are the main types of strike and are the basis of all other strikes.[169]

5.2.3 Mittelhaw

Later masters such as Mair, Meyer and Sutor recognise a third basic strike: a horizontal cut. This is not quite as useful as the Oberhaw and the Underhaw, as it tends to leave a fighter significantly more open to receiving a hit, but it can prove valuable from time to time.

---

[169] Anonymous. *Hs.3227a* (trans. Keith Farrell, 2013), 24r

5.3 Common Thrusts with the Sword

5.3.1 Zorn Ort / Zornhaw Ort

This can be translated simply as the "wrath thrust". The technique begins as a normal Zornhaw, to control the centre line, and it performs the dual roles of threatening the opponent and defending the person who uses the technique. Once the Zornhaw lands in the bind, the point of the sword can shoot straight forwards and stab the other person in the face. However, if the other combatant is putting pressure on the bind, then the correct method by which to execute the Zorn Ort is to wind up into an Ochs-like position to control the bind and then to thrust from above.

> When you cut in against him with a Zornhaw and he defends himself and holds backs, strong against you in the bind, so become strong again against him in the bind and push up with the 'strong' of the sword against the "weak" of his sword, and wind your hilt high in front of your head, and thrust down from above into his face.[170]

Jörg Wilhalm's treatise is unusual in that it shows how to perform the Zornhaw from both left and right high guards,[171] and also shows how to perform the Zorn Ort from both sides.[172] There is a section in Peter Falkner's manual that, depending on the translation, might suggest that the Zornhaw can be done from both sides.[173]

---

[170] Ringeck. *MS Dresden C487* (trans. Keith Farrell, 2011), 19v-20r.
[171] Hutter. *Codex I.6.2º.2*, 6r-6v.
[172] Ibid., 2r-2v.
[173] Falkner. *MS KK5012*, 2v.

5.3.2 Thrusts from Absetzen and Ansetzen

When making a defence with a longsword, "setting aside" a strike by using the Pflug or Ochs guards, the sword's point is angled forward in this position. The natural – and expected – follow up motion should be a thrust from these positions of defence.

> When someone stands against you and holds his sword as if he thinks to thrust at you from below, stand against him in the Plough guard [*Pflug*] on your right side and give yourself an opening on the left side. If he then thrusts from below to this opening, wind with your sword against his thrust, out to your left side, and step towards him with your right foot, so you can hit with your point as he misses.[174]

5.3.3 Other Common Thrusts

There are not very many thrusts that bear their own name. The Zorn Ort is in fact the only named thrust in the core of Liechtenauer's system. Talhoffer gives some of his techniques their own names, such as "Fryes Ortt"[175] and "Geschrenckt Ortt",[176] but his teachings have a different flavour from the other treatises that illustrate the core of Liechtenauer's teachings.

However, in Ringeck's treatise and the anonymous treatise found in the *Codex Danzig* and the *Goliath*, many sequences use thrusts to defeat the opponent if and when a cut fails. Thrusts are a very important part of the longsword system of fighting, much more important than perhaps many people believe, but they receive less limelight than the various strikes because of their simple and relatively uncomplicated nature.

If it is possible to make a thrust when fighting with the longsword then the opportunity should be taken!

5.4 Slices with the Sword

5.4.1 Abschnyden

"Slicing" is a type of technique in the Liechtenauer tradition, different from "striking". A strike is a technique in which the sword begins by not touching the opponent, and is then swung into or at the opponent, or at the weapon. A slice is a technique where the sword begins with the edge already in contact (or almost in contact) with the opponent, and the edge is then drawn or pushed forcefully across the opponent in order to cut him.

---

[174] Ringeck. *MS Dresden C487* (trans. Keith Farrell, 2011), 40r-40v.
[175] Talhoffer. *Codex icon.394a*, 6v.
[176] Ibid., 10v.

Ringeck describes four slices, one of which is also an example of Hende Druck ("hand pressing"), a concept that is will be explained in the following section. The first slice is done when the opponent rushes in close and goes high with his hands:

> Understand this: when he rushes in towards you and goes high up with the arms and wants to overpower you with strength from above against your left side, wind your sword and fall with the long edge with crossed hands under his hilt against his arm; and press
> upwards with the slice. Or if he rushes in towards your right side, fall with the short edge against his arm and press upwards as before.[177]

The second slice is done when you bind strongly with your opponent and allow him to attempt to strike around to the other side with his sword:

> When with a strike or in some other manner you bind strongly with his sword; let him pull his sword away from you and strike from above to your head. Then wind your sword with the hilt in front of your head and slice his arm from below; and thrust the point in the slice down into his breast.[178]

This slice is a defensive movement to hamper and prevent an incoming strike, leaving your sword a strong position from which to finish the fight:

> When someone binds your sword to your left side and strikes round from the sword with the Zwerhaw or suchlike to your right side, spring with the left foot out to his right side away from the strike, and fall with the long edge from above over both arms. Do this on both sides.[179]

5.4.2 Hende Druck

This technique is known as "hand pressing", something which is similar to slicing. The intention is to press or push the opponent's arms, wrists, hands or sword in a particular direction both in defence and to prepare for a different follow-up attack. This is also one of the "four slices" described by Ringeck:

> When you can come with an under-slice to his arm when he rushes in, so that your point goes out to his right side; press upwards with the slice. And in the pressing, spring with the left foot out to his right side, and wind your sword with the long edge from above over his arms so that your point goes out to his left side; and press his arms away from you.[180]

---

[177] Ringeck. *MS Dresden C487* (trans. Keith Farrell, 2011), 45r.
[178] Ibid., 45r-45v.
[179] Ibid., 45v-46r.
[180] Ibid., 46r.

5.5 The "Secret Strikes" of the Liechtenauer Tradition

5.5.1 Fünff Hewen / Verbognehewen / Meisterhauwen

Liechtenauer identified a set of "five strikes" (also described as "secret strikes" by masters such as Ringeck and "master strikes" by masters such as Meyer) with which a combatant may strike an opponent, may "break" or "displace" any of the core guards, and may also keep himself safe as the technique is performed. In this book these strikes will be referred to as the "secret strikes" since this is consistent with Ringeck's nomenclature.

These strikes are the Zornhaw, Zwerhaw, Schaitelhaw, Schilhaw and Krumphaw. All but the Zornhaw can be used to "break" a particular guard; the very nature of how the technique is performed causes one of the core guards to fail in its job of protecting the body. The Zwerhaw breaks Vom Tag, the Schaitelhaw breaks Pflug, the Schilhaw breaks Alber, and the Krumphaw breaks Ochs. The Zornhaw is recognised as one of the most powerful and useful strikes that a combatant can throw, and while it does not break a particular guard it does keep a combatant safe as the strike is launched towards an opponent.

Although the secret strikes can be used to break guards, they should not be regarded as a foolproof method of doing so. Performing a secret strike against a solid guard that is held by a well grounded opponent is an action that is likely to fail; instead a secret strike should be used during the vulnerable period when an opponent is moving from one guard to another and has not yet fully assumed a strong guard. Sometimes a secret strike can pull an opponent out of a strongly held safe position but this is much more difficult to achieve. Thus, using the secret strike properly is an issue of correct timing as well as correct technique.

The following descriptions provide a brief overview of the five secret strikes described by Liechtenauer's markverse.

5.5.2 Zornhaw

The Zornhaw, or "wrath strike", is an Oberhaw that cuts from high on the right and down into the bind. The Zornhaw strikes with the long edge and is an excellent strike to use as the Vorschlag: it combines power and speed with long range, so it allows a combatant to strike swiftly at the opponent from a reasonable distance. If the opponent does not react swiftly enough then the strike can of course be delivered to an opening on the opponent's head or torso, but the masterful nature of the strike lies in its ability to bind strongly and to control the centre line between the combatants, threatening to thrust with the Zorn Ort as described earlier in this chapter.

The Zornhaw is one of the simplest strikes that can be employed in a fight, and thus there is little information in the manuscripts about precisely how one should perform it. Different historical masters used the technique for different purposes and executed it in different fashions, to the point where (from a modern overview of the system) the following has been said of the strike:

> Here's what we actually know: the Zornhau is one of the five (3227a, Anonymous), or maybe six (Leckeuchner, Falkner), but potentially seven (Hutter), or perhaps even ten (Wurttemberg) mastercuts (or just two, like in Kal). It's a defensive action--except in Meyer and Sutor, where it's an offensive action. It's a long-edge strike--except in Wurttemberg where it's a short-edge strike. It starts at the roof and cuts to the hanger, except in the later sources where it starts in Zornhut and cuts to Weschel. Depending on which treatise you trust, it's either a cut that is supposed to kill the opponent, a cut that's supposed to deflect and chamber a thrust (which then kills the opponent), or a purely thrusting action that sort of resembles a cut. It may be the same as the Zornort or a different technique entirely. (Paurnfeyndt sadly doesn't have much to add to this except to state that the Zornhau is the counter to Zwerchhau, but he muddies the waters quite nicely on a lot of other techniques.) And that's just the resources that have been translated into English.[181]

There is however a lot of information about when and how one might use a Zornhaw in different situations, which reflects its simple and multi-purpose role in a combatant's repertoire. The *Hs.3227a* states that when:

---

[181] In 2011, Michael Chidester posted this description to the HEMA Alliance forum in this thread: *http://hemaalliance.com/discussion/viewtopic.php?f=3&t=1210&p=14371#p14366*

> When a descending strike is made from the shoulder, Liechtenauer calls this the Wrath Strike. When you are under pressure, no other technique is as ready as this cut from above, launched from the shoulder at the man.[182]

While this commentary only says that a Zornhaw is an Oberhaw from the shoulder, Ringeck gives a little more information: in his gloss, the Zornhaw is an Oberhaw struck from the right shoulder with the long edge.[183] This makes sense as we are told in many different manuscripts not to fence from the weaker side as we seek the Vorschlag; we are also told that the Zornhaw is good for seeking the Vorschlag. For a left-handed combatant it would make more sense to launch the Zornhaw from the left shoulder.

Jörg Wilhalm shows a Zornhaw originating from the left shoulder of a right-handed combatant,[184] but this is the only manuscript that shows this technique specifically.

Peter Falkner wrote that the Zornhaw could be done on both sides, with or without a step.[185] He does not say that it originates from the left shoulder, merely that the strike can be done on both sides of the body.

5.5.3 Zwerhaw

The Zwerhaw has several English translations, such as "cross strike", "crosswise strike", "slant strike", "thwart strike" and "dwarf strike". It is a high strike that ends in something similar to an Ochs position. This technique lands with the short edge if striking from right to left and finishes in a left, arms-uncrossed Ochs-like position. It lands with the long edge if striking from left to right, and finishes in a right, arms-crossed Ochs-like position. A Zwerhaw can be thrown as either an Oberhaw (descending at a slight angle into the target), as an Underhaw (coming up at a slight angle into the target), or as a Mittelhaw (coming horizontally into the target, parallel to the ground).

This strike can be used as a Vorschlag, particularly against Vom Tag (the guard that this technique is able to break). The Zwerhaw can also be used Indes ("instantly"), or as a Nachschlag, either if used as a follow up to your

---

[182] Anonymous. *Hs.3227a* (trans. Keith Farrell, 2013), 23r-23v.

[183] Ringeck. *MS Dresden C487* (trans. Keith Farrell, 2011), 19r.

[184] Hutter. *Codex I.6.2º.2*, 6v.

[185] Falkner. *MS KK5012*, 2v.

first strike, or to counter an Oberhaw. A good example of this is drawn from Ringeck's treatise:

> The Zwerhaw counters all strikes that cut down from above. When he cuts down against you towards your head, spring with your right foot against him away from the cut [so diagonally forwards and to the right], out to his left side. And in the spring turn your sword - with the hilt high in front your head, so that your thumb comes under [the blade] - and cut him with the short edge against his left side. So you catch his cut in your hilt and strike him in the head.[186]

This is a valuable strike, since it can work at a very close range, or it can be used from further away as a method to close the distance under some kind of cover. The ability to launch into a Zwerhaw from a bind, from a displacement or parry, or from a feint or other kind of action is a very useful ability. Indeed, Joachim Meyer wrote that it is one of the most important strikes to understand in the study of fencing:

> The Zwirch is one of the foremost masterful techniques with the sword. You should know that if the Zwirch did not exist in modern fencing then we would lose half the art, especially when you are under the other man's sword, where can no longer use your long cuts through the cross.[187]

5.5.4 Schaitelhaw

The Schaitelhaw, or parting strike, is an Oberhaw that cuts straight downwards along a vertical line, and is designed to break Alber. The Schaitelhaw strikes with the long edge and the hands should be kept high while executing the cut.

> When he stands against you in the fool's guard, cut with the long edge from the "long parting" from above and down; and keep the arms high in the cut, and hang with the point in against the face.[188]

On the surface this should be one of the simplest secret strikes to perform, and seems like it should be a lightning fast strike to the scalp or face of one's opponent, but sometimes this is not very applicable in free sparring due to the threat of a rising strike to the hands by the opponent.

If the opponent is well trained and has a healthy sense of self-preservation (so is more likely to defend himself against your Schaitelhaw than try to cut your hands and gain a double-hit result) then your task is easier. Throw a very fast vertical cut at his head from a close enough distance and you stand a very good chance of either hitting him in the head or bringing him out from his low guard, into a new position that is vulnerable to slicing.

---

[186] Ringeck. *MS Dresden C487* (trans. Keith Farrell, 2011), 27r.
[187] Meyer. *Gründtliche Beschreibung der Kunst des Fechtens* (trans. Keith Farrell, 2013), 1.55r.
[188] Ringeck. MS Dresden C487 (trans. Keith Farrell, 2011), 32v.

If the opponent is twitchy, and might attack your hands rather than defend properly against your attack, launch the strike within correct distance and make it look like it is intended either to hit the head or to result in a thrust to the face; but stop short, before your hands come into range of a rising cut from the opponent. If the opponent leaves Alber to defend himself from this cut, then the strength of Alber is broken. If he does not have a strong sense of self-preservation and cuts at your hands instead of defending himself, the fact that you stopped outside his effective range should mean that your hands should remain safe. This keeps you safe, and in the case of either reaction, the recipient has been brought out of his couched Alber position.

Both options are good. With either method, if he parries with a lower hanger then you can start to apply your knowledge of winding in the bind to defeat this new position. If he parries by raising his hands high in front of his head, moving into a Kron position, an Ochs position, or really anything that takes the hands high, then you can disengage from the bind and slice across the exposed underside of his forearms. Alternatively, you could disengage and thrust him in the now-exposed torso, but this is a much less safe option than slicing to control the arms due to the concept of an "after blow" from the opponent.

5.5.5 Schilhaw

The Schilhaw, or squinting strike, is an Oberhaw that strikes with the short edge. It provides excellent defensive options against powerful incoming attacks:

> The Schilhaw is a strike which counters cuts and thrusts from the buffalos – those who take their mastery through violent strength. Do the strike like this: when he cuts in against you from his right side, you should also cut from your right side with the short edge with the arms outstretched against his cut, against the "weak" of his sword and cut him on his right shoulder.[189]

It has many different uses, from countering cuts and thrusts to defeating guards and stationary positions:

---

189 Ibid., 31r-31v.

Mark well; to strike the Schilhaw breaks the long point; and then do this: when he stands against you and holds the point with outstretched arms towards the face or chest, so stand with the left foot forward and search with the gaze against the point, and pretend as if you want to strike against the point; and strike powerfully with the short edge above his sword, and thrust with the point along with the blade against the neck with a step towards him with the right foot.[190]

An interesting note from this passage is that the first part of the Schilhaw is done without a step. Simply by twisting the body, the strong of your sword can be brought to bear with the short edge coming down onto the weakest part of the opponent's sword, making for a very effective displacement. This motion also lines up the point of the sword ready for a thrust, and the coiled nature of the body after the twist would make for a very explosive motion. Once the initial displacement is performed, the thrust is then accompanied by a step with the right foot, finishing the sequence.

This method of performing the strike makes it much more successful than trying to chain the cut to a full step. By remaining stationary and twisting the body in the strike, a much better distance is maintained, and the resulting range allows for the follow-up thrust or any other follow-up action to be made and pursued without coming ineffectively close to the opponent.

The most effective way to think about the Schilhaw from the earlier sources in the Liechtenauer tradition is that it is a two-action movement: the first action is the twist and short edge strike for defence and/or to gain a better structural position with relation to the opponent's sword; the second action is the thrust or whatever else needs to happen next. It is not a "single time" action, at least not according to Ringeck's treatise.

---

[190] Ibid., 32r.

5.5.6 Krumphaw

The Krumphaw has a number of English translations, for example: "crooked strike", "crooked cut", "arc strike", "crumple strike", "crumple hew", and "folded action". There have been many interpretations of this technique by different HEMA groups, and there has been much rivalry over whose method is the best, or which version is THE correct Krumphaw. The authors believe that all such arguments are pointless, because the medieval masters described different versions of the Krumphaw for different situations. We are told in the manuscripts that the Krumphaw can be used as a defence (to set aside incoming attacks), as a counter cut (getting out of the way of an incoming attack while striking at the opponent Indes) or as an offensive method for breaking both the Ochs guard and the position of Lang Ort.

Rather than trying to interpret this technique as a particular strike done in a particular fashion, it is better to think about it like this: the Krumphaw is not a single strike, rather it is a concept of how to strike. The best description for this technique comes from the *Hs.3227a* where the author writes that:

> Note that the Crooked Strike is a cut from above, performed by stepping far to the one side while cutting crookedly to the other side.[191]

To put it simply: the Krumphaw is a technique that involves a step and a strike, where the two components are not necessarily chained together by the normal rules. For example, normal practice is to step with the right leg when cutting from right to left from the right shoulder; one version of the Krumphaw comes from the right shoulder, cutting left to right, but still stepping with the right leg, resulting in a "crooked" strike with crossed hands.

Different manuscripts illustrate or describe the strike as performed with the long edge,[192] the short edge[193] or with the flat.[194] In different situations, different methods of performing the Krumphaw are more effective. It is worth experimenting with the different methods to find what works best for the majority of situations, and then gradually to add the other methods to your repertoire over time.

[191] Anonymous. *Hs.3227a* (trans. Keith Farrell, 2013), 25v.
[192] Anonymous. *MS Germ.Quart.2020*, 18r.
    Meyer. *Gründtliche Beschreibung der Kunst des Fechtens,* 1.12v.
[193] Talhoffer. *Codex icon.394a*, 11r.
    Kal. *CGM 1507*, 66v.
    Anonymous. *MS Germ.Quart.2020*, 19r.
    Sutor. *New Künstliches Fechtbuch*, 17.
[194] Anonymous. *Hs.3227a*, 25v.
    Ringeck. *MS Dresden C487*, 51v-52r.

5.6 The Wechselhaw

Beyond Liechtenauer's five secret strikes, we have also decided to include one of the tradition's supplementary techniques: the Wechselhaw. Although this technique is not as central to the tradition as the secret strikes, it is still a technique worth knowing.

The Wechselhaw is first referenced in the *Hs.3227a*, in the section on fighting multiple opponents;[195] however, sadly, no technical details are given about this strike. The next manual to deal with the Wechselhaw is the 1467 manuscript by Talhoffer,[196] which is not of much help either. The illustration simply depicts a combatant standing in a Wechselhut position with the phrase Wechselhaw written next to him. From this, we cannot tell if he is in the starting point, end point, or even a mid point of the Wechselhaw.

Paulus Hector Mair was the first to write something specific about the Wechselhaw, saying that:

> In the zufechten, when you come to the man and want to strike with the wechsel, put your left foot forward and strike up from below towards his face with the short edge remaining above. Step with your right foot and cut in from above with the long edge to the right side of his head.[197]

Joachim Meyer developed a more general view of the Wechselhaw:

> The Wechselhaw is nothing other than working before the man with the cuts, from one side to the other, from above to below, back and forth, to confuse him.[198]

So Meyer wrote that the Wechselhaw is a combination of two strikes, one of which travels in one direction, and is followed by a second strike that travels back in the opposite direction. This means that the example given by Mair fits the definition given by Meyer, but it is only one of four possible variations for the Wechselhaw, which are as follows:

- an Oberhaw to the opponent's upper left opening followed by an Underhaw to his lower right opening;
- an Oberhaw to the opponent's upper right opening followed by an Underhaw to his lower left opening;
- an Underhaw to the opponent's lower left opening followed by an Oberhaw to his upper right opening;
- an Underhaw to the opponent's lower right opening followed by an Oberhaw to his upper left opening.

If we use the example from Mair, we can see multiple reasons why one might use the Wechselhaw. The first and simplest reason is that if one strikes with an Oberhaw into a low guard such as Alber, the opponent might step

---

[195] Anonymous. *Hs.3227a*, 44v.
[196] Talhoffer. *Codex icon.394a*, 2v.
[197] Mair. *MS Dresden C93* (trans. Keith Farrell, 2013), 54r.
[198] Meyer. *Gründtliche Beschreibung der Kunst des Fechtens* (trans. Keith Farrell, 2013), 1.14v.

backwards, requiring a follow-up with an Underhaw to be able to land a strike. Alternatively, the Wechselhaw might be thrown on purpose as a two-part technique: one might strike with the Underhaw in order to beat the opponent's sword out of the way, clearing the way for one to strike him with the Oberhaw. We see this application of the Wechselhaw used in the third play of Lignitzer's sword and buckler treatise, and a similar follow-up action in the section of Ringeck's treatise that discusses defensive "sweeps".

The Underhaw might also be a feint, or Fehler, in order to draw the opponent's attention and defences down towards his lower left, in order to be able to strike him more easily in his upper right. Finally, one might strike with the Underhaw with the intention of hitting the opponent, but if he seeks to bind, one might then Durchwechseln in order to strike to the other side.

Please note that there are many more of these supplementary techniques, which, while being useful, are not central to the Liechtenauer tradition. We hope to release more information about these supplementary techniques on our blog, Encased in Steel, or in future publications.

5.7 Binding and Winding with the Longsword

5.7.1 Binden, or the Bind

The bind occurs when your sword and your opponent's sword meet and cross each other during a fight. Usually one combatant throws the Vorschlag in the form of some kind of strike and the other combatant binds with this strike in some defensive manner so that the strike will not land. The bind is a major element in Liechtenauer's style of longsword, and learning how to bind safely and then to control the bind is of utmost importance.

5.7.2 Winden, or the Wind

When two blades meet each other in the bind, the combatants do not stand straining at the swords like we see in most Hollywood films. Rather, the two combatants "wind" or move their blades in the bind, maintaining contact between the two blades, seeking an advantageous position from which they may strike, thrust, slice, close to grapple or even to disengage safely. During the wind the two blades stay in contact with each other, because if one blade was to be removed from the bind then the other blade could lash out and strike without hindrance. Thus when a bind occurs, the combatants wind their weapons until one combatant is able to establish dominance and either progresses the fight to the next stage or ends the fight with an attack made from the bind. Learning how to wind your sword effectively in the bind is also a skill of critical importance in Liechtenauer's style.

5.7.3 Vier Hengen, or the Four Hangings

The Vier Hengen are the "four hangings". These are simply the two Oberhangen and the two Underhangen, the Ochs and the Pflug on both sides. These positions allow one to defend one's self capably in close quarters, and can bind with any attack coming for any of the four openings.

5.7.4 Fühlen, or Feeling

When one's sword binds with an opponent's sword, it is important to be receptive to how the bind feels. Every time either combatant does anything in the bind, the other combatant can feel this through the connection between the two swords. When you bind with your opponent it is crucial that you ascertain whether he is being strong or weak in the bind. If you merely assume that he is going to be weak and thus try to be strong to beat him, then he may well be strong and thus defeat your naive attempt at winding.

The masters wrote in many of the manuscripts that it is important to gauge your opponent in the bind, to feel what he is trying to do. For example, the Hs.3227a tells us that:

> When it is a trial of strength against strength, the stronger fighter will always win. That is why Liechtenauer's art is a true art, where the weaker one may win more easily by using his art correctly, and the stronger one will have more difficulty winning by strength alone. Else what good would be this art? Therefore, learn how to feel in fencing. Liechtenauer says that one should learn how to feel. "Instantly" is a very sharp word: if you find yourself bound with your sword upon the sword of another, feel if he is weak or if he is strong, then Instantly make your decision and understand what is most appropriate for you to do, according to the art that has been taught before. If you do this, then he will not be able to disengage his blade from yours while remaining safe.[199]

---

[199] Anonymous. Hs.3227a (trans. Keith Farrell, 2013), 22v.

In a similar fashion, Ringeck advises that:

> You shall carefully learn and understand Feeling [*Fühlen*] and the word Instantly [*Indes*], because these two things go together and are the highest art of fencing. When someone beings the other with the sword, so in the same moment when the swords come together you shall already feel if he has bound strongly or weakly. And as soon as you have felt this, think of the word Instantly [*Indes*]: that is to say, that in the same instant you feel this, you should deftly work against the weak and against the strong with the sword to the nearest opening. So he will be beaten before he has time to understand this.[200]

5.7.5 Indes, or "Instantly"

When a bind occurs, the combatants have a chance to use Fuhlen and to feel what is happening in the bind. The ideal response to a bind is to feel swiftly how much pressure both combatants are exerting on the centre-line and then to make the appropriate wind or other response. Acting "Indes" is to apply Fuhlen immediately when a bind develops and to choose the appropriate response to the bind depending on the results of feeling the pressures. By acting Indes a combatant can take advantage of any incoming attack and steal (or retain) the initiative.

In the Liechtenauer tradition, masters prized this skill highly; in fact they regarded it as one of the most important aspects of fighting. Ringeck stresses heavily just how important the skill of Indes can be for a fencer:

> In all bindings with the sword you shall think of the word "Instantly" [*Indes*], because "Instantly" doubles and "Instantly" mutates, "Instantly" runs through and "Instantly" takes the cut, "Instantly" wrestles, "Instantly" takes the sword from him, "Instantly" does in the art all that your heart desires. "Instantly" is a sharp word, which cuts all those fencers who do not know something about the word. And the word "Instantly" is also the key, whereby all fencing art is unlocked.[201]

5.7.6 Acht Winden, or the Eight Windings

The Acht Winden are the "eight windings" and these are ways of maneouvering and working around an opponent's sword in the bind. A bind can happen with your sword on the right of the opponent's sword (for example, both combatants launch an Oberhaw from the right shoulder, the blades crossing each other between the combatants), or it can happen with your sword on the left of the opponent's sword (for example, the same scenario but the strikes come from the left shoulder instead of the right shoulder). A bind can happen on either side.

---

[200] Ringeck. *MS Dresden C487* (trans. Keith Farrell, 2011), 38r.
[201] Ibid., 39r.

The bind on the right can happen in either an Oberhengen an Underhengen position, so two possible binds on the right. Likewise there can be two possible binds on the left. This gives four possible binding positions:

- a bind on the right in an upper hanging;
- a bind on the right in a lower hanging;
- a bind on the left in an upper hanging;
- a bind on the left in an under hanging.

From these binding positions, combatants should use Fühlen to feel what is happening in the bind. If there is no pressure and the opponent is not contesting the line between the two combatants then no winding is needed and a swift thrust will suffice to win the exchange. If there is some sort of pressure then an appropriate winding action needs to be performed, and a wind can be a "hard" wind into the bind to produce more leverage and control of the line or it can be a "soft" wind away from the opponent's pressure, yielding the line in order to achieve a more advantageous position while still maintaining contact with the opponent's sword. Since a combatant can only wind "hard" or "soft", two types of action can be made from each of the four possible binding positions, giving eight possible winding actions.

Each winding action has several possible ways by which it can be implemented, and these are described in the various manuals. The theoretical concept of eight possible winds underpins all examples of winding in the manuals, and it is easiest to understand this concept as follows:

- binds can happen on the right or on the left;
- you can bind in an upper hanging or a lower hanging;
- this gives four possible binding positions;
- from each binding position there can be a "hard" wind or a "soft" wind;
- this gives eight possible winding actions.

5.7.7 Drei Wunder, or the Three Wounders

The Drei Wunder are the "three wounders", which are the three ways to wound someone with a longsword while in a bind. These are the "haw" (or strike), the "stich" (or thrust) and the "schnitt" (or slice).

Each of the eight windings can culminate in each of the Drei Wunder: each winding can result in a strike, a slice or a stab. So there are in fact twenty-four actions that can come from winding, as Liechtenauer remarks in his markverse:

> He who acts well and counters correctly, who understands completely, and who breaks apart everything with the three wounders, who uses the hangers well and correctly, and winds when these occur, with eight windings; who considers correctly that each of the windings are threefold, so I mean that there are twenty and four, when counted from both sides.[202]

---

[202] Ibid., 123v.

5.7.8 Hart, or Strong

A combatant is said to be "strong" in the bind if his sword is binding with pressure against the opponent's blade. Another way of looking at the concept is to say that a combatant is "strong" if he is contesting the "centre-line" in the bind, an imaginary line that runs between the two combatants. It can sometimes be a good thing if you are strong in the bind, as it allows you to exert influence over your opponent's sword by winding against him. However, it is not always the best idea to be strong in the bind, as sometimes the opponent will be able to use your strength against you, in which case your strength will leave you undefended and unprepared against a sudden and unexpected technique from the opponent.

5.7.9 Weich, or Weak

A combatant is said to be "weak" in the bind if his sword is binding against an opponent's blade but without any real resistance. This is often a good thing, as it allows one to turn the opponent's strength and resistance against him and to set him up to create an opening, but it is a difficult skill to master. Being weak in the bind is no better and no worse than being strong in the bind; it is important to use each skill at the appropriate time.

5.7.10 Duplieren, or Doubling

When you bind with your opponent, you can try to "double" and perform another strike against him. However, you need to remain in the bind; if you remove your sword from the bind to strike again, then he will be able to thrust his point into you before you can complete your strike. To perform Duplieren successfully, you must stay in the bind, so wind your sword in such a manner that your long edge or short edge strikes either of his upper openings. For example, we are told by Ringeck that:

> When you strike in with a Zornhaw or another Oberhaw and he defends himself strongly, immediately [*Indes*] push your sword's pommel in under your right arm with your left hand, and cut him in the bind over the face with crossed hands, between the sword and the man. Or cut him with the sword in the head.[203]

---

[203] Ibid., 24r.

Pushing the pommel under the right arm has the effect of turning your sword so that your long edge is no longer touching his sword; instead your short edge is now in contact with your opponent's sword. This twist also has the effect of cutting with the long edge across your opponent's face; his sword is prevented from striking you, because you have maintained the bind and wound your sword safely into your opponent. This is just one example of how to perform Duplieren from the bind, and is an example of a "soft" winding action that results in a strike.

Note that Duplieren or "doubling" actions (which are good) should not be confused with "double hits" (which are bad).

5.7.11 Mutieren, or Mutating

In a similar fashion to Duplieren, you can "mutate" from the bind and thrust into one of his lower openings as part of the winding. For the same reasons as for Duplieren, you do not want to leave the bind to perform the new strike; you need to maintain contact with the opponent's sword to prevent him from striking you first. Ringeck gives an example of mutating where he tells us that:

> When you bind against his sword with an Oberhaw or another such strike, so wind the short edge against his sword and go up with the arms; and hang your sword blade over his sword on the outside and thrust into him through the lower opening.[204]

When the two blades bind, your long edge is touching his sword. By pushing your hands up to what is effectively an Ochs guard on the left side of your head, your blade remains in the bind against his but your short edge becomes the edge in contact with his sword. Assuming this position prevents his sword from being able to strike you, and allows you to thrust powerfully down into his gut from the Ochs, always maintaining contact with his sword so that he is unable to prevent your strike and also unable to hurt you. Again, this is just one example of how to use Mutieren, and it is an example of a "hard" winding action that results in a thrust.

5.7.12 Zucken, or Tugging

Sometimes when the opponent binds with your sword, you want his blade to pass to the side and clear the way for you to strike him. If the opponent binds so hard with you that you cannot even effect a "soft" wind against him, then simply twitch or tug your blade away from his, leaving the bind, and strike to his head from the other side.

---

204 Ibid., 24v.

When you come against him in Zufechten, strike powerfully from above from your right shoulder in against his head. If he binds against the sword with a parry or suchlike, step in closer to him in the bind and tug your sword up and away from his and cut back down against him on the other side of the head.[205]

5.7.13 Durchwechseln, or Changing Through

The Durchwechseln is a disengaging action. If the opponent is just about to bind with you then simply drop your point slightly, and then raise it up again on the other side of the opponent's sword. It is a good idea to make this semi-circle as small as you can, because the smaller it is, the faster it will be, and so the harder it will be to counter.

> You shall learn carefully to change-through. When you strike or thrust in against him in Zufechten and he tries to bind against the sword with a cut or a parry, let the point sweep through under his sword, and hurt him with a thrust to the other side, quickly find one of his openings.[206]

5.7.14 Durchlauffen, or Running Through

Durchlauffen is the process of entering from the bind into wrestling at the sword, or "Ringen am Schwert". Ringeck recommends that when you run-through, you push up with the sword, and let go with the right hand, while still holding onto the pommel with the left hand. As the sword hangs over your back, it will remain between you and your opponent's sword as you move into grappling distance.

> When one rushes in closer to the other and goes up with the arms and wants to overpower you above with the strong; go up with your own arms and hold your sword by the pommel with the left hand over your head, and let the blade hang behind over your back.[207]

5.8 One-Handed Attacks

5.8.1 Das Gayszlen, or The Whip

This is an interesting one-handed technique shown by Hans Talhoffer.[208] No information is given about the technique, merely a single illustration that shows a combatant swinging a low attack towards an opponent's leg. The left hand remains on the pommel of the sword and the right hand is taken from the grip of the sword; this allows the strike to gain the extra range necessary to make a strike to the legs effective (according to the principle of Überlauffen as described earlier).

---

[205] Ibid., 41r-41v.
[206] Ibid., 40v-41r.
[207] Ibid., 42r.
[208] Talhoffer. *Codex icon.394a*, 6v.

5.8.2 One-Handed Thrust

One of the manuals by Jörg Wilhalm shows a one-handed thrust.[209] In a similar fashion to Talhoffer's Gayszlen, the left hand remains on the pommel of the sword and the right hand is removed from the grip to allow for a greater thrusting range. The right shoulder is pulled backwards and away from the sword, allowing the left shoulder to advance further forwards. This has the dual benefit of allowing the thrust to gain a little extra range and also taking the bulk of the body away from possible retribution or counter attack.

5.8.3 General Note

It can be very tempting to perform lots of one-handed strikes when sparring with the longsword, especially under pressured situations like tournaments. However, it is important to recognise that Talhoffer's Gayszlen and Wilhalm's thrust are the only two examples of one-handed strikes in the extended Liechtenauer tradition of unarmoured longsword fencing, and are absent entirely from Liechtenauer's markverses or the early glosses that expand and explain the markverses. That means that strikes such as these were not important techniques, nor were they described by most of the masters in this tradition; therefore they should not be overused and abused in sparring.

5.9 Further Strikes by Other Masters

Other masters such as Joachim Meyer and Jobbst von Württemberg described other strikes in their treatises. Furthermore, some masters mention more than five secret strikes. The reason why these other strikes and additional secret strikes are not discussed in this work is that the authors of this book are not familiar enough with the description and application of these techniques to be able to write about them in a comprehensive and responsible fashion. Furthermore, this book is intended to be a reference guide for the method of longsword taught within the Academy of Historical Arts; since these techniques are not taught (yet) within the Academy by any of its instructors, it would be a matter of guesswork to write about these techniques and how they work, and that would be irresponsible. A future revision of this book may contain such information as the knowledge of the Academy's instructors and researchers grows over time.

The omission of techniques is a decision that has not been taken lightly. In the interests of producing a useful and well-researched book as a reference guide for the organisation in which the authors teach, the best option was simply to go ahead and explain the techniques that are already well understood and that are taught regularly as part of the syllabus. The authors hope that readers will respect this decision.

---

[209] Hutter. *Codex I.6.2º.2*, 23v.

Chapter 6: Ranges and Timing

6.1 Ranges of the Fight; or Onset, War and Withdrawal

The two stages of a fight are Zufechten, or the onset (literally the to-fight) and the Krieg, or the war. It is important to be aware of range and distance when fighting, as doing something at the wrong range is clearly going to be much less effective than doing it at the proper range.

6.1.1 An Old Interpretation of Stages

These two stages have sometimes been interpreted in the following fashion: that Zufechten is the range at which you must step to hit the opponent and Krieg is the range at which you can hit your opponent without stepping.[210] This is an early and simplified interpretation and is probably not quite correct.

To look at the ranges in this fashion means that all the emphasis is put on Krieg; by the definition in the previous paragraph, Zufechten is the range where nothing directly offensive can happen because neither opponent can hit the other without moving to a different range. This approach does not hold up to scrutiny, because if this is the case, then by striking one must enter Krieg, or the strike will fall short and not hit.

In the *Hs.3227a* it is said that winning the Vorschlag is very important,[211] which seems to advise that it is good to strike as soon as possible and therefore to enter Krieg as soon as possible (by the above definition of the ranges). However, this contradicts the gloss by Sigmund Ringeck that cautions the reader not to rush into Krieg: "you shall not be too hasty to go into Krieg".[212] How can one seek to strike first, and at the same time not rush into Krieg, if striking automatically moves the fight to within Krieg distance?

Further, Ringeck tells us "Krieg is nothing other than the windings in the bind".[213] By this definition, Krieg is not the distance within which one can land a hit without a step; rather it is the act of winding. Zufechten must therefore be all the actions we can make before winding occurs.

While this old interpretation was a good first step on the route to understanding the ranges, it is not quite correct enough to be a good guideline for combatants. Therefore, the authors of this book would like to present a newer theory about how the different ranges can be conceptualised.

---

[210] Christian Tobler. *Fighting with the German Longsword* (Chivalry Bookshelf, 2004), 25.
[211] Anonymous. *Hs.3227a*, 14v.
[212] Ringeck. *MS Dresden C487* (trans. Keith Farrell, 2011), 21r.
[213] Ibid.

6.1.2 Definition of Krieg

Ringeck has a full lesson devoted to cautioning a student about rushing into the close quarter combat that is Krieg:

> Note to practice these:
> cut, thrust, postures - weak and hard.
> "Instantly" and "Before", "After"
> without rush. Do not hurry into the war.
> When the war occurs
> above, below he is shamed.
>
> When one binds against your sword with a cut or thrust or anything else, you must find out whether he is soft or hard in the bind. And when you find this, you will "Instantly" know what is best to do, to attack him with "Before" or "After". But in the attack you shall not be too hasty to go into the War [Krieg], because this is nothing other than the windings in the bind.
>
> Perform close combat like this: when you cut against him with a Zornhaw, when he defends himself quickly, you shall go up in an orderly fashion with the arms and wind against his sword with your point in against the upper opening.
>
> If he defends against this thrust, stand in the winding and thrust with the point into the lower openings.
>
> If he follows further after the sword in self-defence, go under his sword with the point through to the other side and hang your point over in against the other opening on his right side.
>
> In this way he will be cut down in close combat both above and below, because you (unlike he) can perform the movements correctly.[214]

What this lesson shows is that Krieg should happen "in an orderly fashion" and that one should "not be too hasty to go into the War". The markverse by Liechtenauer himself cautions that one should "not seek the War prematurely". This is quite a strong admonishment not to rush into the "windings in the bind" but rather to ensure that the skills are present to handle it competently, and also that the action of moving to Krieg fits the tactical situation in the fight and is the most suitable option given the circumstances. It also implies that moving to the windings or continuing to wind is not always the best idea, which is of course borne out by techniques like Durchwechseln (changing through; leaving the bind and thrusting at the other person) or Zucken (tugging; leaving the bind and cutting at the other person) or Durchlauffen (running through; closing to grapple from a bind).

Therefore Krieg happens when the two combatants bind and start to wind against each other.

---

[214] Ibid., 20v-22r.

6.1.3 Definition of Zufechten

The Zufechten is more difficult to define precisely. Here are some snippets from Ringeck's gloss that discuss the Zufechten and what to do in different scenarios.

> When you come against him in the Zufechten you shall not await his attack, and neither shall you wait to see what he is thinking about doing to you. All fencers who are hesitant and wait for the incoming attack, and do nothing other than to ward it away, they gain very little joy from this sort of practice because they are often beaten.[215]

In the above quote, the Zufechten is used to describe the sort of range at which either combatant can attack each other; the Zufechten is also therefore the stage of the fight when the combatants are coming to each other and before the first attack is launched.

> When you come against him in the Zufechten, if you are right-handed and want to strike him, you must not throw your first cut from your left side. That is because this is weak and cannot bring strength to bear if he binds the strong of his blade against you. Therefore, cut from your right side, so you can be strong and skillful in the bind and can do as you will.[216]

In the above quote, the Zufechten is used to describe the point in time when a combatant considers throwing the first strike.

---

215 Ibid., 13r-14r.
216 Ibid., 14r-14v.

In the next quote, the Zufechten is described as the sort of range at which a combatant may throw a strike or a thrust and land a hit upon the other person.

> Always pay attention to the openings in the Zufechten. His openings you shall skillfully seek without danger: with thrusts with the outstretched point [*Lang Ort*], with travelling after and with all other techniques. And do not pay heed to what he tries to do with his techniques against you, but fence with belief and throw strikes that are excellent and that do not allow him to come at you with his own techniques.[217]

In a similar fashion, the next quote shows that the Zufechten is when you may launch a strike at the opponent:

> When you come against him in the Zufechten; when it becomes suitable for you, spring against him and cut with the Zwerhaw against the lower opening on his left side. This is called "to strike against the plough".[218]

This quote shows that the Zufechten is the distance at which a feint is successful because it can be made to look like it will land, to be threatening, therefore enticing a response from the opponent:

> When you come against him in the Zufechten, pretend that you want to cut him with perhaps an Oberhaw to his left side. In this manner you can strike him underneath however you want and defeat him.[219]

In fact, the Zufechten can be the distance at which you can feint twice before landing your real strike:

> This is called the double feint, because in the Zufechten you shall be misleading two times. Do the first like this: when you come against him in the Zufechten, take a spring with the foot against him and pretend that you will cut with a Zwerhaw against the left side of his head. And change the direction of the cut, to the right side of his head.[220]

The next quote shows that the Zufechten can still refer to a very short and close distance where Überlauffen works and is effective:

> In the Zufechten, when he aims for a lower opening with a cut or a thrust, do not defend yourself against it. Rather, wait until you can reach over him with a strike from above against the head or a thrust from above, so he will be defeated by you, because all Oberhaw and all high attacks reach further than lower strikes.[221]

This quote again supports the notion that the Zufechten is the range at which the first strike or thrust is launched:

---

[217] Ibid., 22v-23v.
[218] Ibid., 27r-29v.
[219] Ibid., 29v-31r.
[220] Ibid.
[221] Ibid., 39v.

80

When you come against him in Zufechten, strike powerfully from above from your right shoulder in against his head.[222]

The next quote helps to show that the Zufechten is the range at which the combatants close and begin to consider the options with regard to launching the first technique:

> You shall learn carefully to change-through. When you strike or thrust in against him in the Zufechten and he tries to bind against the sword with a cut or a parry, let the point sweep through under his sword, and hurt him with a thrust to the other side, quickly find one of his openings.[223]

This quote shows that the Zufechten extends to a further distance as well, not just in close or at initial striking distance:

> Before you come too close to him in Zufechten, set your left foot forwards and hold the point towards him with outstretched arms towards the face or the chest.[224]

This last quote is very interesting because it suggests that the Zufechten is the range at which winding can happen. Since windings are part of Krieg, this suggests that the act of Krieg does not necessarily remove the fight from the Zufechten.

> A Zufechten from the setting-aside.

> When you fence with someone and when you come close to him, you should stand in the Plough [Pflug]; and then use windings deftly from one side to the other so that you are always keeping your point in the one place.

> And from this you can use the parries, it is the distance; and furthermore you can become stronger with the true edge and from there use all aforementioned techniques. You can also set aside cuts and thrusts and counter them simply with windings and seek the opening with the point.[225]

In fact, the best way to think about a fight is to realise that in order for the fight to actually happen, one combatant must take the fight to the other person. Until an exchange is initiated, the two combatants are looking for the opportunity, looking for openings, testing the waters, perhaps offering feints and generally preparing for whatever exchange happens. This is part of the Zufechten, as it is the "to-fight", the precursor to the fight. Then one combatant takes the initiative and launches the Vorschlag; this is also the "to-fight" as the fight is being taken to the other person. The opponent may bind and start winding, and this then becomes Krieg, but can also still be part of the "to-fight".

Why is everything before an exchange and then during the delivery of an exchange all part of the Zufechten or "to-fight"? Well, until the opponent is

---

[222] Ibid., 41r-41v.
[223] Ibid., 40v-41r.
[224] Ibid., 123r.
[225] Ibid., 51r-51v.

defeated, everything involves taking the fight to him and continuing to employ attacks, counter attacks and offensive winds.

After a hit has been delivered, a combatant may need to extricate himself from the exchange, keeping himself safe on the way out just in case the opponent was not entirely disabled during the exchange. Unfortunately the earlier sources do not say much about that part of the fight, but some of the later treatises discuss the third range of the fight: the Abzug, or withdrawal from the exchange.

6.1.4 Abzug, or Withdrawal

A third potential range is Abzug, which can be translated as withdrawal, or end.

> I call the beginning the "to-fight" [*Zufechten*], when two opponents who face each other begin to fight. The middle I call the "hand-work" [*Handtarbeit*], where one remains in the bind with his opponent and presses him with nimble work. The end is called the "withdrawal" [*Abzug*], where one withdraws safely and cuts away any threats.[226]

Here Meyer equates the Abzug as being a range of equal importance to Zufechten and Krieg, but neither Liechtenauer's verses or the glosses of Liechtenauer mention the Abzug, and the Abzug is not mentioned until the 16th century, so its existence as a named concept seems to be a late addition to the art. Potentially it was part of the training given by the earlier masters to their students, but unfortunately the earlier sources do not discuss it in detail. Alternatively, perhaps the earlier masters placed greater emphasis on controlling an opponent's blade in the bind, and using the Drei Wunder in such a fashion that the opponent's body would also be controlled, thus negating the possibility of a stage of active combat beyond the Krieg.

Meyer provides a short chapter on the Abzug in his manual.[227] A brief summary of the subject would conclude that attacks do not always work as planned, sometimes an individual will need to extricate himself from the situation, and this should be done in a safe fashion so that no hits are taken on the way out. This is an important part of fighting and should not be ignored. Striking an opponent is but a single facet of winning a fight and coming out unscathed at the end; a safe withdrawal is vital.

---

[226] Meyer. *Gründtliche Beschreibung der Kunst des Fechtens* (trans. Keith Farrell, 2013), 1.1v-1.2r.
[227] Ibid., 1.23r-1.23v.

6.2 Timings of the Fight; or Before, After and Instantly

6.2.1 Vor

The Vor is the "before" in an exchange during a fight. The combatant who takes the initiative and strikes first is in the Vor and is in control of the "before". This is usually advantageous, as the person who strikes first is more likely to land a hit, all things being equal. Of course, all things are very rarely equal, but the German masters often praised the Vor and suggested that combatants attempt to control it. Controlling the Vor is obviously beneficial and we are told that:

> The concept of "Before" means that a skilled fencer should always make the first strike.[228]

If the two combatants separate after exchanging strikes, then it becomes important for both combatants to again strive to control the next Vor. This process repeats every time there is a separation between exchanges.

It has often been interpreted that the exhortations to win the Vor in sources such as the *Hs.3227a* and the *Codex Ringeck* mean that combatants should be aggressive and do nothing but attack. This is quite clearly wrong and at odds with the advice in the sources that cautions fighters against being too hasty, that suggests waiting to see what the other person does, that talks about being sensible and in control of the fight.

To this end, fighters should not seek to be "aggressive" but rather "assertive".[229] An assertive fighter will control the fight, will control the initiative, and can force the opponent to make mistakes. An assertive fighter will still think about his own defence and take care, will not rush into close distance for Krieg, will employ good technique and skill without having his mind clouded with aggressiveness. Aggressive fighters are called buffalos and are ridiculed in the sources; one can be assertive and land fast and powerful strikes without letting the opponent come to blows.

The Vor is important in a fight and initiative should be seized in a safe fashion wherever possible, without reducing combatants to aggressive buffalos who do nothing but press the attack.

6.2.2 Nach

The Nach is the "after" in an exchange during a fight. After one combatant has taken the initiative and has controlled the Vor by throwing the first strike, the fight moves into the "after" and the combatants must strive to

---

[228] Anonymous. *Hs.3227a* (trans. Keith Farrell, 2013), 20r.
[229] Keith Farrell. "'Aggressive' vs 'Assertive' for Martial Arts." *Encased in Steel*, 2013. http://historical-academy.co.uk/blog/2013/02/11/aggressive-vs-assertive-for-martial-arts/

control the Nach. During the Nach, the combatant holding the initiative may change; the person who threw the first attack may not always retain the initiative, sometimes the other combatant may steal it. In the same way as the combatants strive to take the initiative; they also strive to control the Nach. Controlling the Nach effectively is important regardless of which combatant took control of the Vor at the beginning of the exchange.

The Nach persists until the combatants break apart after the exchange, at which point they must strive once more for the Vor.

6.2.3 Nachreissen

Nachreissen is often translated as "travelling after" or "following after" and is the term given to an attack that follows after an opponent's attack. Ringeck gives an excellent example of following after an opponent's strike:

> When he cuts forward towards you, misses and continues to cut down towards the ground with his sword, follow after him with an Oberhaw to his head before he can bring up his sword again.[230]

One example of Nachreissen is where you wait until your opponent throws an attack towards you, move out of the way just enough so that the attack misses you, then throw your own attack before the opponent can recover to defend himself. This requires a high level of skill in distance and timing, and also a high level of self-discipline to move back just enough without going too far (as this would mean that you would be too far away to hit with your own attack).

Another example of Nachreissen is when an opponent moves from one guard position to another, creating an opening where his sword used to be; striking to this opening, just as he vacates the spot, is another way to employ the concept of Nachreissen.

6.2.4 Indes

Indes is the time when both combatants act simultaneously, or where one combatant reacts almost instantly when the opponent does something. While the sources say that Indes is a very important skill and that "this word cuts sharply",[231] it is important not to take this as justification to swing without thinking as soon as you notice your opponent is doing something. Indes is a skill as well as a moment in time; it is not a case of "see, swing, and hope".

---

[230] Ringeck. *MS Dresden C487* (trans. Keith Farrell, 2011), 37r.
[231] Ibid., 38r.

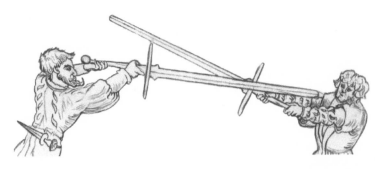

Where Indes really comes into play is in the bind. When your opponent comes with an attack and you respond with some kind of technique that creates a bind, there are a few things that can happen. If you do your defence and then stop, your opponent can continue his sequence of attacks and press his advantage, pushing you on the defensive and making the situation much less safe for you. If you do your defence and riposte at him immediately, then a "double hit" will occur if he continues his sequence of attacks. These two examples show neither stopping nor acting without due assessment of the situation are good ways to handle a bind.

The best way to handle a bind is to pause for just long enough to see what the other person plans to do, and then to pick an appropriate response that both keeps you safe and endangers the other person. If he fails to react to your threat and keeps swinging his attack at you, then you stay safe and you hit him. If he sees the threat and aborts his attack in order to deal with the threat, then you have managed to keep yourself safe and you have stolen the initiative away from the attacker; the initiative is now yours, and you may press your advantage with further attacks to which he must react defensively.

It is worth including Indes in the "timeline" of a fight, because Indes is the moment where the person controlling the Vor stops controlling the Vor, and where the person who was in the Nach now gains the initiative and the opportunity to press forward.

6.3 Essay: Distance and Range in Practice

by Keith Farrell

It is important for practitioners to learn about distance and range and to employ these concepts correctly in practice when drilling, exercising or sparring with the longsword. It is often the case that people who interpret from the treatises are unable to make a technique or a sequence actually work in practice; often the problem is not with the technique or sequence but rather with the distance or range of the attempted application.

Two key terms need to be defined: distance and range.

Distance is the physical distance between you and your opponent. If your opponent is so far away that he cannot hit you and you cannot hit him then you are at a safe distance, whereas a closer distance will mean that strikes will be able to land.

Range is similar but a lot more specific: each technique has a different range. A long technique like a long edge Oberhaw will have a long range; a short technique like a punch has a short range, and a missile weapon like a throwing axe will have a very long range indeed! Distance is an absolute concept: you might be five feet away from your opponent, or three feet away, or two feet away. Range is a relative concept: a kick has a longer range than a punch; a thrust with the point of a sword has a longer range than a strike with the pommel.

For example, every practitioner of German longsword will at some stage learn about the Zwerhaw, and will practice using it as a defence against an Oberhaw. While this can generally be made to work with plenty of success in drilling, it often does not transfer over so well to sparring. Why is it so difficult to make it work in sparring when it can be successful in every drill?

Imagine a simple Zwerhaw training practice. One combatant attacks with an Oberhaw, the defender catches it with a Zwerhaw and uses the technique to hit the attacker on the side of the head, as described by Ringeck:

> When he cuts in from above against your head, spring with the right foot against him away from the cut, out to his left side. And as you spring turn your sword – with the hilt high in front of your head, so that your thumb comes under – and cut him with the short edge against his left side.[232]

In the drill, the combatants may become engrossed in what is happening with the swords, and may forget to pay attention to what their feet are doing and the distances at which techniques are to be performed. Students often start quite far apart in drills, then drift closer together until the drill can be done almost without stepping at all, because it is easier that way. This behaviour continues until the situation reaches a point where the attacker throws an Oberhaw that, were it to land, would hit with the middle or perhaps even the strong of the blade. At this distance the defender can still execute a perfect Zwerhaw without needing to move forwards at all, just taking a short step to the side. This might not

---

232 Ibid., 27r.

seem like a major problem to students, since surely this does still train the method by which a Zwerhaw can beat an Oberhaw, and surely the combatants get the gist of how to do this?

Well, not particularly. When sparring, people tend to adopt a much greater distance from each other than when drilling. Assuming the scenario occurs in sparring where one combatant takes the role of attacker and throws an Oberhaw, the defender should in theory be able to counter it with a Zwerhaw. After all, that is what Ringeck's gloss says, and what many other glosses say. However, if the only thing the defender has practiced is to make a small step to the side then he will find in sparring that his own counter may fail to reach the attacker. All that happens is that the Oberhaw is caught on an Ochs-like parry without threat to the attacker, so the attacker can simply wind up and or leave the bind or do whatever he wants to retain the initiative. Or even worse, because the defender is not doing the Zwerhaw properly, he receives a painful hit to his hands! The attacker then wins the exchange and the defender is left discouraged because the technique that had been practiced meticulously did not work.

The key thing here is that when the combatants did their drilling, not enough attention was paid to the distance between them. If the drill had started with greater distance, so that both combatants had to close towards each other before the exchange happened, then the attacker would be training a proper Oberhaw that reaches out to find the opponent, and the defender would be training a Zwerhaw that would serve the dual purpose of defending the head and also landing a cut on the attacker. This is preferable, and all that it takes to reach this higher level of training is to ensure that drilling combatants start each drill further apart from each other.

This example shows that techniques, sequences and interpretations can work in drilling due to the somewhat co-operative nature of the exercise, but can also fall apart when tested under pressure due to the lack of understanding of distance and range at which everything should occur.

When studying a system of historical European martial arts, it is important to be aware of distance and range. Things simply do not work at the wrong distance and so practitioners should develop an understanding of these concepts. Rather than discarding an interpretation because it fails to work under pressure, it might be worth looking at the interpretation in terms of the distance and range at which it is being performed – when these concepts are addressed, interpretations that seemed to be deficient may well become valuable and highly effective in sparring, as well as in drilling.

Chapter 7: Principles of Attacking

This chapter is a compilation of several articles that have previously featured on Encased in Steel, the weekly blog of the Academy of Historical Arts. The following articles by Alex Bourdas have all been highly edited, revised, and compiled to form this essay:

- "Principles and the Book of Martial Power";[233]
- "Rushing Forward, and Besieging";[234]
- "The Defensive Advantage, the Vor, and the Master Strikes";[235]
- "Fuhlen, Indes and Managing Defensive and Offensive Advantages".[236]

Also contributing to this essay is the article "Principles Behind the 'Master Strikes'"[237] by Keith Farrell.

If you have read the original articles, please note that there will be some differences, for example, this essay refers to the Offensive and Counter-Offensive Principles, as opposed to the Offensive and Defensive Principles mentioned in the blog. These changes were made due to a greater understanding of martial principles on the part of the authors since the blog articles were written, and for easier comprehension.

Principles are "a fundamental law or truth upon which other techniques or actions are based".[238] They are universal to all martial arts, regardless of origin or focus, and therefore if any practitioner says "one of the principles of my style is..." then he is using the term principle incorrectly, because a principle "that exists in one style but not another, or in some styles but not all, cannot be a true principle as we define it here".[239] It could be argued that in some ways principles are more important than any techniques, as techniques are simply particular physical movement patterns designed to follow the principles. The techniques can be interchanged with one another; however, this does not hold true with principles.

To give an example, the Vier Versetzen are a grouping of techniques informed by the principle of Simultaneous Offence and Defence (i.e. that ideally you should both defend yourself and attack the opponent at the same time). We are told that we should counter Vom Tag with the Zwerhaw and

---

[233] Alex Bourdas. "Principles and the Book of Martial Power." *Encased in Steel*, 2012. http://historical-academy.co.uk/blog/2012/05/18/principles-and-the-book-of-martial-power/

[234] Alex Bourdas. "Rushing Forward, and Besieging." *Encased in Steel*, 2012. http://historical-academy.co.uk/blog/2012/06/22/rushing-forward-and-besieging/

[235] Alex Bourdas. "The Defensive Advantage, the Vor, and the Master Strikes." *Encased in Steel*, 2012. http://historical-academy.co.uk/blog/2012/08/10/the-defensive-advantage-the-vor-and-the-master-strikes-2/

[236] Alex Bourdas. "Fuhlen, Indes and Managing Defensive and Offensive Advantages." *Encased in Steel*, 2012. http://historical-academy.co.uk/blog/2012/10/12/fuhlen-indes-and-managing-defensive-and-offensive-advantages/

[237] Keith Farrell. "Principles Behind the 'Master Strikes'." *Encased in Steel*, 2012. http://historical-academy.co.uk/blog/2012/07/13/principles-behind-the-master-strikes/

[238] Steven Pearlman, *The Book of Martial Power*, 2008.

[239] Ibid.

we can infer that this is because it counters an Oberhaw, the most likely response from Vom Tag. However, this is not the only method you could use to counter Vom Tag. You could also use a regular Oberhaw or Underhaw depending on the timing or range, or you could thrust from Alber up into Ochs (providing the same cover that a Zwerhaw gives), and of course there are many other options. The Zwerhaw happens to be the exemplar of the principle of Simultaneous Offence and Defence for this situation; however, as long as that principle remains in effect, any other technique could be used.

The study of principles is important because the fechtbücher, and in particular the *Hs.3227a*, attempt to explain the principles. However, a brief study of what is being said about the principles can lead to drawing martially unsafe and possibly invalid conclusions. These quotes seem to imply that Liechtenauer tells combatants to rush forward and attack, no matter what:

> It is correct when, with courage, you rush forwards against the opponent with the first strike, as you will be told hereafter.[240]

> Strike at him thrice, powerfully, and rush in regardless of whether you hit or miss.[241]

> And when you fight for real, you should use the teachings described before, and you should make the first strike.[242]

> Fight with a clear mind, and always make the first strike.[243]

> Therefore Liechtenauer does not particularly care for the guard positions. He cares much more than you try to win the first strike.[244]

---

[240] Anonymous. *Hs.3227a* (trans. Keith Farrell, 2013), 16v.
[241] Ibid., 18r.
[242] Ibid., 27v-28r.
[243] Ibid., 29v.
[244] Ibid.

However, practical experience will quickly show that continually rushing forward to attack regardless of circumstance will often result in either a double-hit or the defender taking advantage of a principle that we will refer to as the Counter-Offensive Advantage.

The principle of the Counter-Offensive Advantage states that when a movement is being executed, the person carrying out that movement is vulnerable to a counter-attack. This can be seen most clearly when attacking, since when you move to attack you will often create a defensive deficiency. That might be by creating an opening on yourself, by giving the opponent an opportunity to use the energy and momentum that you have generated with your attack against you, or because you are so focused on the attack that your mind is less able to deal with threats elsewhere.

There is no clear description of the Counter-Offensive Advantage in the fechtbücher. In contrast, the Offensive Advantage is much more clearly explained. The Offensive Advantage principle states that no defence has 100% defensive effectiveness, and that the greater the number of attacks that are launched, the greater the likelihood of the defender being struck.

> And due to that which is taught here, I say to you truly, that the opponent cannot defend himself without danger. If you have understood this then you will not let him make his strikes.[245]

Due to the Offensive Advantage, a fencer should not try just to defend himself without also offending the opponent.

> All fencers who are hesitant and wait for the incoming attack, and do nothing other than to ward it away, they gain very little joy from this sort of practice because they are often beaten.[246]

This means that you should try to minimise the extent to which your opponent can use the Offensive Advantage against you, i.e. you should minimise the number of attacks your opponent can launch at you. To do that, you need to offend opponents in such a way that they cannot attack you. From this point of view, offence and defence become inextricably linked: you attack the opponent in order to defend yourself.

This requires a bit of a shift in attitude. If you decide that you're just going to hit the opponent for the sake of doing so, you may hit him, and may very well get hit yourself in the process. Attacking the opponent for the sake of hitting can give you defensive deficiencies, and therefore does not follow martial principles correctly. However, attacking the opponent in order to defend yourself is rather different.

At times you may not be able to attack the opponent directly. Sometimes you may be forced to block or parry an opponent's strike. It is worth noting that a block may have differing degrees of offensiveness. A block may be entirely defensive, with no offensive characteristics. A block that lets you

---

[245] Ibid., 17v.
[246] Ringeck. *MS Dresden C487* (trans. Keith Farrell, 2011), 13r-13v.

defend yourself while creating an opening in the opponent could be considered to be mostly defensive, but also to be partially offensive. An example of this sort of technique may be a block or parry that places your point on-line, threatening the opponent. A technique which blocks an incoming attack and at the same time strikes the opponent may be considered to be equally defensive and offensive, and may be ideal, but this is not always safe[247] or possible. However, even if you cannot strike the opponent while you are defending yourself, you may still be able to improve your positioning relative to his, and so you would still have followed the principles of combat correctly, regardless of style or school. So if you are forced to block or parry against an opponent's attack, you should do so in such a way that you set up a follow-up attack for yourself.

In summary, you should use the Offensive Advantage against your opponent to reduce his ability to use the Offensive Advantage. When the opponent attacks you, you should use the Counter-Offensive Advantage against him in order to offend him (either directly or indirectly) so that you can prevent him from carrying out further attacks against you. Additionally, when you attack the opponent, you should do in such a way that you reduce his ability to use Counter-Offensive Advantage, i.e. you should not leave yourself open for an easy counter-attack when you attack.

There are various strategies that can be used against an opponent in order to meet these goals:

1) Waiting for an opponent to create a defensive deficiency within his actions, and then taking advantage of that before he regains his ability to use the Counter-Offensive Advantage;

2) Prompting an opponent to create a defensive deficiency within his actions, and then attacking as above;

3) Using one of Liechtenauer's "secret strikes" against an opponent.

It is worth noting however that these strategies are not entirely separate, and there is a degree of overlap between these strategies, as will be seen later.

If an opponent is in a stable guard, and so has the ability to make use of the Counter-Offensive Advantage, you can wait for him to make a mistake and create an opening in his defence. Some people might think that simply waiting for an opening is wrong, and that you must act first. After all, Ringeck wrote:

---

[247] Differing weapons lengths can make counter-attacks in opposition more or less safe (i.e. defending against an attack and striking the opponent at the exact same time). Greg Mele wrote an excellent article called "Counterattacks with Opposition: The Influence of Weapon Form" in SPADA: an Anthology of Swordsmanship, in which he argued that normally you need a blade of 36 inches or greater to safely carry out counter-attacks in opposition. For more information on sword lengths within the Liechtenauer tradition, see the essay entitled "Length of a Longsword" within this book. This is just one example of how an external factor can present a practical reason not to try to reach 100% offensiveness in all techniques, and there are many other possible reasons, which this essay sadly does not have time to explore.

All fencers who are hesitant and wait for the incoming attack, and do nothing other than to ward it away, they gain very little joy from this sort of practice because they are often beaten.[248]

One could use passages like this to support the idea that you should never wait for an opening into which to attack, and that you should always be going forward with an attack. However, the passage specifically mentions fencers who are hesitant and who do nothing other than ward away incoming strikes. It talks about fencers who are too hesitant to attack, who just sit back and only try to defend themselves, without attacking the opponent. This overly defensive behaviour exacerbates the problems of the Offensive Advantage, since if you try to do nothing but defend against all attacks, eventually one attack (at least) will break through your defence.

This is quite a different scenario to waiting for an opponent to attack and then (when the opening presents itself) counter-attacking in an attempt to end the encounter quickly. This approach reduces the opponent's ability to make use of the Offensive Advantage.

In Żabiński's translation of the Hs.3227a, the phrase "Do not strike at the sword, but wait for the openings" appears four times.[249] If the opponent is in a stable guard, it is perfectly permissible to wait for those openings to appear. If the opponent stumbles in his footwork, if his guard creeps out of the correct position, or if he attacks you improperly, then he loses his ability to make use of the Counter-Offensive Advantage, and you can take advantage of that fact and hit him.

However, you also want to be able to create a defensive deficiency in the opponent. If the opponent creates this deficiency himself, then you can take advantage of that. However, you cannot rely on the opponent making a mistake by himself. Sometimes it will be necessary to trick the opponent into creating that defensive deficiency. If we look at a source from outside the Liechtenauer tradition, we can see that other sources may have useful information to tell us about the principles of offence. The MS I.33 has a rather complex system of "custodiae" and "obsessi". Dr Forgeng translates these terms as "ward" and "counter", respectively; however, "obsesseo" may also be translated as "to besiege".[250]

This alternate translation is interesting, and leads to a rather useful analogy. Imagine you are leading an army to take a city. You march your army quickly and reach the city while it is still unprepared. The gates are open and there are no archers or gunners posted on the city walls. Assuming that this is not a trap, the smart thing to do is to rush your army through the open gates as quickly as you can and take the city before they can raise their defences.

[248] Ringeck. MS Dresden C487 (trans. Keith Farrell, 2011), 13r-13v.
[249] Anonymous. Hs.3227a (trans. Keith Farrell, 2013), ff. 18v, 23v, 29v & 65r.
[250] Stephen Hand posted the idea to Sword Forum International here:
http://www.swordforum.com/forums/showthread.php?86907-I.33-translations

However, if the city was prepared, or your army was simply too slow in reaching it, the gates may be closed. If the gates are closed, it is no use aggressively rushing forward with your army, because your army will just break on the walls. So if the defences are prepared, you must lay siege to the city, and break down their defences in some way. The analogy isn't perfect (starving your enemy into submission isn't normally an option in one-on-one combat, for instance), but it illustrates a point very well.

It is the authors' understanding of the *MS I.33* system that if your opponent does not adopt a proper guard or ward, you can just hit him. If he does adopt a proper ward however, you are forced to adopt an "obsesseo" and besiege him until there is an opening for you to attack safely. This process tells us something very interesting about the principles involved in offence.

If the defender is not ready to defend himself, then it is safe and sensible to rush forward and attack relentlessly (in fact, if the defender is not ready to defend himself, we would say that it is not martially valid to give him time to make himself ready instead of attacking him). If the defender is ready, then he can use the Counter-Offensive Advantage against you. Therefore, if he is ready, you must besiege him so as to put him in a position where he can no longer make use of the Counter-Offensive Advantage effectively.

Let us give an example of this for longsword. It is written that if the opponent is in Alber, you should attack with a Schaitelhaw.

> When he stands against you in the fool's guard, cut with the long edge from the "long parting" from above and down; and keep the arms high in the cut, and hang with the point in against the face.[251]

This is a bit problematic unfortunately, and to show why, let us look at what happens if the opponent is still moving into Alber. If you are fighting an opponent, and he is still in the process of moving into Alber, then he has lost his ability to make use of the Counter-Offensive Advantage, as his sword is moving away from yours. If he moves down into Alber, then to defend himself he must stop the motion of the sword and then reverse it, giving you a short space in time when you can attack safely. So if he is still in the process of moving into Alber, you should rush forward bravely and strike him, as we are told in the Nachreissen section.

> When he cuts against you from above and he continues downwards towards the ground with his sword, follow after him with an Oberhaw to the head, before he comes up with the sword.[252]

The key part of that quote is "before he comes up with the sword." As he is moving into Alber, you must strike quickly, before he has a chance to regain his ability to make use of the Counter-Offensive Advantage.

However, returning to the Schaitelhaw example, if he is standing in Alber, then he has the ability to make use of the Counter-Offensive Advantage since his sword is in a position where he can easily move to defend himself. It is

---

[251] Ringeck. *MS Dresden C487* (trans. Keith Farrell, 2011), 32v-33r.
[252] Ibid., 37r.

widely agreed that Alber works well as a provoking sort of position. If your opponent stands in Alber (or any low guard, really), he is probably trying to entice you to try to hit him, so that he can cut up into your hands or into your strike to deflect it. Once your strike is deflected, you lose your ability to make use of the Counter-Offensive Advantage, and you are open to attack.

It is tempting to treat this case in the same way as in the Nachreissen example, and to think "he is in Alber, therefore I should hit him in the head". However, attempting to use the Schaitelhaw against a person who is ready for it, in a position to defend against it, and who in fact wants you to strike at him, is very unsafe. If he stands in Alber, and you strike directly to his head, even if he doesn't deflect your strike, there is nothing to stop him from cutting up into your hands. Yes, you may have hit him on the head, but you haven't kept yourself safe, and may be hit on your hands.

Note that what Ringeck says is "cut down … and hang with the point in against the face". We are not actually told to hit the opponent with the Schaitelhaw, we are told to hang the point in against his face. If someone is in Alber, you can throw the Schaitelhaw from just out of distance so that it does not actually hit him, so that your hands are not in danger from his possible cut from Alber, and so that your point is threatening his face. If you do this, the opponent will naturally raise his hands to defend himself and so he will come out of Alber. This means that he was in a strong defensive guard, but you have drawn him out of that guard by besieging him.

After moving out of Alber, he will not have the same capacity to make use of the Counter-Offensive Advantage as before, and you can take advantage of his movement with the Counter-Offensive Advantage yourself.

It was explained above that the Counter-Offensive Advantage could be used to attack an opponent when he attacks you; however, this principle holds true for all forms of movement, not just attacks. Therefore when he moves in any way, he may create an opening into which you may attack safely. In the case of Alber, if he raises his hands to a high Kron or Ochs position, you can perform a Schnitt by coming up from below, against his now-exposed hands and arms.

It is also possible for you to remove an opponent's ability to use the Counter-Offensive Advantage by binding with his sword and claiming the centreline. So you can prevent the opponent from taking advantage of the Counter-Offensive Advantage by removing him from a position from which he can counter attack easily, or by placing your sword correctly between yourself and your opponent so that it protects you from any counter attack. The other secret strikes (the Zornhaw, Krumphaw, Zwerhaw and Schilhaw) can all be used to do this.

Let us consider the Zwerhaw first; it is an interesting strike that can be used to beat Vom Tag. Using the Zwerhaw has a major advantage over the Oberhaw in terms of being able to break Vom Tag: the motion naturally terminates in a high Ochs-like position, which protects you above your head and out to the side from where any retaliatory strike is likely to come. We are told that "the Zwerhaw takes away that which comes from above" and we are given a description of how one might use the Zwerhaw to defeat an incoming Oberhaw from above or from the right shoulder.[253] There are various ways to perform this technique, some more successful than others, but the end result is that the Zwerhaw should always be able to beat an Oberhaw by the placing of the sword in an Ochs-like position in the path of

the incoming strike, at the same time as (or swiftly followed by) a counter-strike with the short edge of the sword.

The Zwerhaw may be used to break Vom Tag for this very reason. By swiftly leaping forward and right, throwing the short edge out at the head or arms of the opponent and terminating in an Ochs-like position, the strike lands on the person in Vom Tag. If the person in Vom Tag reacts and throws a retaliatory Oberhaw, this can be intercepted by the Zwerhaw which has been used to claim the centreline and defend the attacker from descending attacks, making it much harder for the opponent to take advantage of the Counter-Offensive Advantage. Even if the person reacts with a strike and moves himself away from your point, you still end in the bind in quite a strong position; even if the Zwerhaw fails to kill the opponent in that one motion, it has still "broken" a strong guard by forcing the opponent out of the position and into an unwanted bind that you will now be able to dominate by using Indes and Fuhlen.

Another secret strike is the Krumphaw. It beats a left Ochs by taking your body off-line, away from the threatening point of Ochs, and casting the point of your sword towards the hands of the person standing in the guard.[254] This can be done by leaping well off to the side, taking yourself away from the opponent so that he cannot strike you; by beating his blade with the Krumphaw to push it

off the centreline, so that his sword is no longer threatening you;[255] or by a combination of these two approaches. This is not the only way to perform the Krumphaw – the different masters describe different ways of doing the strike and in different situations – but this particular method is driven by principle

[253] Ibid., 27r-29v.
[254] Ibid., 24v-27r.
[255] For a demonstration of this, please see the video *Goliath Krumphau* by Dustin Reagan, 2012: http://www.youtube.com/watch?v=wFKRSIQo_pM

rather than being just a single technique that can be used in a given scenario.

The Schilhaw is used to break the Pflug guard. It does this by descending with the short edge of your sword, binding the weak of his sword with the strong of yours, and dropping the point of your sword into his face, neck or chest.[256] Alternatively, the target area can be the opponent's right shoulder, so you strike across the centre of his body and cut him in the shoulder or at the base of the neck. If the strike is made to the right shoulder, then this can place your sword in between the opponent's sword and his head. If the opponent tries to push against your sword, he cannot do so effectively, because your sword is trapped against his neck, and so his ability to use the Counter-Offensive Advantage is drastically reduced.[257]

The Zornhaw works along the same principles. If an opponent cuts in at you with an Oberhaw then you could strike a Zornhaw at it, claiming the centreline and interposing your sword between yourself and the incoming attack. The immediate follow-up is to thrust straight for his face or to wind into Ochs and thrust for the face, depending on whether he is weak or strong in the bind.[258] Or you might use Zucken or Umbschlagen or Duplieren or Mutieren or any other suitable technique. The first part of the motion keeps you safe, and then once you have secured your safety, you make an appropriate motion to strike at the nearest opening.

The secret strikes improve your positioning relative to the opponent (either by physically moving off the centreline, denying him control of the centreline, or both), making it harder for the opponent to use the Counter-Offensive Advantage. They also allow you to use the Counter-Offensive Advantage effectively against the opponent via Fuhlen and Indes.

For example, if you attack an opponent with a Zwerhaw, he may defend against it, likely by striking at your sword. This will create a bind position, allowing you to use Fuhlen and Indes to determine what your next action should be. If he is overly strong in the bind, you could safely leave the bind and strike with a Zwerhaw to the other side of his head, while if he is weak in the bind, you could move in to throw him.[259] There are of course other follow-up techniques that you could use; these are just two examples. This tells us that by using sensory perception, you can read the amount of pressure an opponent is using in a bind, and from there execute the next action appropriately.

If he is pushing his sword to his left side strongly in order to defend himself from the Zwerhaw (and therefore has removed his sword from the centreline), he will be less able to defend his right side. You can therefore make use of the Counter-Offensive Advantage to strike to his right side. If he is defending weakly (and therefore has kept his sword close to the centreline), then striking around would leave you open to his use of the

---

[256] Ringeck. *MS Dresden C487* (trans. Keith Farrell, 2011), 31r-32v.
[257] For a demonstration of this, please see the video *"MKDF Shielhau 2011"* by Jake Norwood, 2011: http://www.youtube.com/watch?v=l_hph7_8MHc
[258] Ringeck. *MS Dresden C487* (trans. Keith Farrell, 2011), 19r-20v.
[259] Ibid., 28r.

Counter-Offensive Advantage, and instead you should remain in the bind and keep your sword between your body and his potential threat.

The secret strikes will normally (at least in the authors' opinion) lead to an advantageous bind if they fail to strike the opponent directly. This bind will then prevent the opponent from striking at you directly by exerting control of the centreline, and will allow you to use Fuhlen and Indes to decide correctly which action to use in order to take advantage of the Counter-Offensive Advantage.

The Liechtenauer tradition presents us with several different options for managing the Offensive and Counter-Offensive Advantages. The secret strikes are the most skilful way of doing this. Another good option it to wait for an opponent to remove himself from a stable guard before attacking is also good. Prompting an opponent to remove himself from a stable guard with techniques such as Fehler (feinting) can also be used to defeat the opponent. There are many ways that the Offensive and Counter-Offensive Advantages can be managed, and unfortunately this essay cannot discuss them all. We hope this essay has prompted you to consider the principles of attacking in greater depth.

Chapter 8: Solo Drills and Exercises

8.1 The Flourish of the Hs.3227a

> If you want to fight with someone in school fighting or in plan, and you wish to be courteous, then you should place your sword a little in front of you. Then go to the Barrier Guard on both sides, and seek openings on both sides with your good footwork. Then move to the lower hangings, also on both sides, with proper footwork. Then do the upper hangings on both sides with good footwork. Then make the cross strike on both sides, again with good footwork. You should always step and move the sword to the other side at the same. If you move to the left side, then step forward with the right; and do the opposite on the other side. And by doing this when you approach him, then you will do in play what is good to do for real.[260]

The *Hs.3227a* gives us one of the few examples of a solo drill from the sources. This is a flourish, an activity that should be done before a sportive match or sparring. This may have been intended as pre-match entertainment for those watching, to give them a prelude to the sort of techniques they could expect to see during the match. It might have served to frighten the opponent, and it has been commented that this would fit in with a long tradition of Germanic warriors trying to intimidate their opponent before a fight.[261] It may also have served as part of a warm-up, but it is likely that a warm-up would have involved more than just one flourish. One final use for it would be solo drilling, in order to practice the techniques contained, similar to the kata of karate. It does not seem that it was used for this purpose in the period, but there is no reason why, as modern practitioners, we cannot treat it as such.

Such a flourish does have a lot of valuable applications for training purposes, and in the Academy of Historical Arts various lessons and workshops have used this flourish as a basis for developing greater understanding of the principles contained within Liechtenauer's system. Some of these workshops have been taught at international events such as Swordfish and HEMAC Dijon, where the points of view and suggested applications of the flourish have met with a lot of interest from people from other HEMA groups.

Members of the French group Artes Belli filmed a workshop about the flourish that Keith Farrell ran at the HEMAC Dijon event in 2012. The video is available online to give people some ideas for how the flourish could be used in training.[262]

---

[260] Anonymous. *Hs.3227a* (trans. Keith Farrell, 2013), 52v.
[261] Jeffrey Hull. "Döbringer Longsword Flourish." HEMA Alliance, 2010.
[262] Keith Farrell, video by Artes Belli, 2012. "The flourish of the Döbringer codex HS 3227a by Keith Farrell": http://www.youtube.com/watch?v=AoK8nvv0nZo

8.2 Meyer's "Four Openings" Drill

Joachim Meyer included in his *Gründtliche Beschreibung der Kunst des Fechtens* a cutting diagram[263] designed to help his students gain fluency in striking to the four openings. We have reformatted this diagram slightly, and present it here.

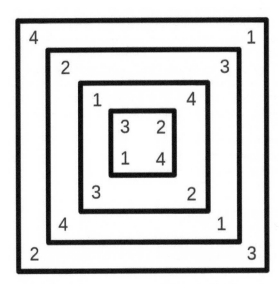

To perform this drill, you strike at the each of the four openings in order of the number presented at each opening. Each square can be used separately or they can all be chained together into one long drill. To clarify, here are the steps if you wanted to use this as one long drill:

Outer square:
     1. Strike an Oberhaw from the right;
     2. Strike an Underhaw from the left;
     3. Strike an Underhaw from the right;
     4. Strike an Oberhaw from the left;

Second square from the outside:
     5. Strike an Underhaw from the right;
     6. Strike an Oberhaw from the left;
     7. Strike an Oberhaw from the right;
     8. Strike an Underhaw from the left;

Second square from the inside:
     9. Strike an Oberhaw from the left;
     10. Strike an Underhaw from the right;
     11. Strike an Underhaw from the left;
     12. Strike an Oberhaw from the right;

---

263 Meyer. *Gründtliche Beschreibung der Kunst des Fechtens*, 1.28r.

Inner square:
>   13. Strike an Underhaw from the left;
>   14. Strike an Oberhaw from the right;
>   15. Strike an Oberhaw from the left;
>   16. Strike an Underhaw from the right.

This drill is very adaptable, as it does not specify how you should make the strikes. You can strike either with the long edge only, with the short edge only, or you could use a combination. You could strike with full-cuts only, or with half-cuts, or with a combination. You could decide to use only the Zwerhaw to strike. You could use any type of footwork you wish, or stay on the same spot if space is an issue. You could run through the entire drill, or you might only use one square at a time. One particularly interesting adaptation is to cut through each number twice before moving on to the next one. So for example, instead of drilling the first square like this:

1. Strike an Oberhaw from the right;
2. Strike an Underhaw from the left;
3. Strike an Underhaw from the right;
4. Strike an Oberhaw from the left;

You could instead drill it like this:

1. Strike an Oberhaw from the right;
2. Strike an Oberhaw from the right;
3. Strike an Underhaw from the left;
4. Strike an Underhaw from the left;
5. Strike an Underhaw from the right;
6. Strike an Underhaw from the right;
7. Strike an Oberhaw from the left;
8. Strike an Oberhaw from the left;

If you strike through each number twice, you could further adapt the drill by alternating which edge you cut with, so for example the first strike in every pair could be done with the short edge, the second strike with the long edge.

In short, this drill is easily adapted, and can be used to train various fluency skills.

8.3 Other Solo Training Methods

If you have access to a pell (a stationary target like a hanging punching bag, or just a post embedded in the ground) then you can practice striking at the pell with your sword. This is a useful exercise for developing fluency with combinations of strikes or even targeting skills. Receiving some kind of tactile feedback at the end of each strike is a distinct advantage of working with a pell over flourishing in thin air.

It is important not to hit a rigid pell too hard while working with it; a pell is not the best method for developing strength, and the repeated shock travelling through the arm after every strike will take its toll on the body.

To make working with the pell more interesting and more valuable, drawing targets in different places on it will allow you to practice accuracy and tip control with single strikes and combinations of strikes. Modifying the pell by rigging an "arm", something like a broomstick handle or a sword projecting out from the pell itself, will allow you to practice entering under cover when you attack, dealing with a sword that is in the way and then landing a strike, a thrust or a slice against the target.

It is worth noting that no source within the Liechtenauer tradition talks about using a pell for practice, so while it is a useful form of exercise if you have access to one, it is not of critical importance to your understanding of the art.

Another useful solo training exercise is to practice cutting with a sharp sword. By cutting soft targets such as cauliflowers, then graduating up to milk bottles filled with water, then graduating up further to clay or rolled and soaked tatami mats, you can practice how to deliver a strike that would actually do damage to an opponent and that would cut through something. When participating in cutting practices, safety should of course be a high priority, since sharp weapons are involved.

It is important to practice cutting as you would practice sparring. If you perform a technique in one fashion while cutting, but you spar completely differently, then you are not training the skill properly. The cutting practice should be an exercise to support the other solo and paired practices and as a validation test to ensure that the techniques can be performed well enough to do real damage.

Again, it is worth noting that no source within the Liechtenauer tradition talks about cutting practices. On Encased in Steel there are various articles about methods of cutting practice,[264] as well as articles about strength and fitness training for swordsmen.[265] If this kind of exercise is of interest to you then it would be worth looking at these articles on the blog.

---

[264] Keith Farrell. "Cutting Concepts." *Encased in Steel,* 2012. http://historical-academy.co.uk/blog/2012/05/25/cutting-concepts/
Ben Kerr. "Benefits of Test Cutting." *Encased in Steel,* 2013. http://historical-academy.co.uk/blog/2013/03/22/benefits-of-test-cutting/
Keith Farrell. "Validating what we do in martial arts." *Encased in Steel,* 2013. http://historical-academy.co.uk/blog/2013/05/03/validating-what-we-do-in-martial-arts/
Alex Bourdas. "Cutting with the German longsword?" *Encased in Steel,* 2013. http://historical-academy.co.uk/blog/2013/04/12/cutting-with-the-german-longsword/
Alex Bourdas. "Cutting with the German longsword, part 2." *Encased in Steel,* 2013. http://historical-academy.co.uk/blog/2013/05/10/cutting-with-the-german-longsword-part-2/
[265] Alex Bourdas. "Fitness for HEMA Part I: Cardio." *Encased in Steel,* 2011. http://historical-academy.co.uk/blog/2011/08/26/fitness-for-hema-part-i-cardio/
Alex Bourdas. "Fitness for HEMA Part II: Strength Training." *Encased in Steel,* 2011. http://historical-academy.co.uk/blog/2011/09/02/fitness-for-hema-part-ii-strength-training/
Alex Bourdas. "Vegetius, double-weight swords, and cutting with the gladius." *Encased in Steel,* 2011. http://historical-academy.co.uk/blog/2011/12/23/vegetius-double-weight-swords-and-cutting-with-the-gladius/

8.4 Paired Drills and Exercises

In general, the Academy of Historical Arts recommends that if students want to practice paired drills, then taking the examples listed in the Codex Ringeck (*MS Dresd. C487*), Codex Danzig (*Codex 44.A.8*) or the Goliath (*MS Germ.Quart.2020*) and using them to set up paired drills would be the best route to follow. These longsword glosses are effectively series of paired drills and exercises, and anything that we could advise as a simple paired drill can often be found in the original manuscripts anyway.

Alex Bourdas. "The nervous system and isometrics." *Encased in Steel*, 2013. http://historical-academy.co.uk/blog/2013/01/18/the-nervous-system-and-isometrics/

Appendix A: Liechtenauer's Zettel

In this appendix is a translation of the Zettel (a.k.a. the markverse or epitome) of Johannes Liechtenauer, as recorded in the Blossfechten treatise by Sigmund Ringeck in the *MS Dresd. C487*.

The Zettel was Liechtenauer's summary of the art of fencing, written as a poem to help his students remember the verses. Liechtenauer wrote a Zettel to cover each of the three subjects of unarmoured longsword fencing, armoured longsword combat, and mounted fighting. The Zettel is all that we have today that was written by Liechtenauer himself. Our other sources are either glosses where later masters explained the Zettel or books of unique material that begins to diverge from Liechtenauer's core teachings. Since the Zettel is the only surviving material written by Liechtenauer himself, and is therefore the earliest written source in the tradition, it is important to be familiar with how the art was summarised and passed down to the other masters in the tradition.

The first version of this translation was prepared by Keith Farrell, based loosely on the Swedish translation by Andreas Engström; the second (and current) version of the translation improved the first attempt, working more directly from the original German text and cutting out the "middle man" of a third language. This English translation of the Zettel is not a literal translation, and is instead intended to read in a more natural fashion in English. Perhaps some of the phrases will read differently to other translations, but it is beneficial to have various options and choices of phrase, in order to stimulate ideas and ways of understanding the text.

> Young knight, learn:
> honour women always, and love God,
> so increase your honour.
> Practice knighthood and learn
> arts that develop you
> and in battle bring honour.
> Wrestle well, understand
> the lance, spear and sword and knife;
> for their use is manly.
> Strike in fiercely!
> Rush in: hit or miss;
> He who has wisdom,
> he will see praise.
> This you shall understand:
> all arts have length and measure.[266]

> If you would show skill,
> go to the left and right with cuts.
> And left with the right,
> is how you fight strongly.[267]

---

[266] Ringeck. *MS Dresden C487* (trans. Keith Farrell, 2011), 11r-11v.
[267] Ibid., 11v.

He who goes after the cut,
receives little joy from his skills.
Cut closely, then do as you will,
so he cannot change through your shield.
Strike to the head, to the body,
do not refrain from swift strikes.
Fight with the whole body,
if you want do this with strength.[268]

Hear what is bad:
do not fence from the left if you are right-handed;
and if you are left-handed,
you are weak from the right.[269]

"Before" and "After", these two things,
from these all other skills spring.
"Weak" and "Strong",
"Instantly", mark well these words.
So you must learn
to work and defend with skill.
If you are easily frightened,
you will never learn fencing.[270]

Learn five cuts from the right hand.
He who can defend himself with these,
he should be praised,
for his art rewards him well.[271]

Wrath strike, Crooked, Cross,
Squinter, with the Parter;
Fool, displacement,
follow after, run over, make the cut,
change through, pull,
run through, slice, press the hands,
hang, and with openings,
strike, catch, sweep and thrust with the point.[272]

He who cuts from above,
threaten him with the Wrath strike's point.[273]
If he recognises this,
so take off above without danger.[274]

Become stronger against
and thrust! If he sees this, take it below.[275]

---

[268] Ibid., 13r.
[269] Ibid., 14r.
[270] Ibid., 14v-15r.
[271] Ibid., 16v-17r.
[272] Ibid., 17v.
[273] Ibid., 19r.
[274] Ibid., 19r-19v.
[275] Ibid., 19v.

Note to practice these:
cut, thrust, postures - weak and hard.
"Instantly" and "Before", "After"
without rush. Do not hurry into the war.
When the war occurs
above, below he is shamed.[276]

In all windings
learn to find the right cut or thrust.
You shall also test
with cut, thrust or slice,
in all exchanges
if you want to beat the masters.[277]

Four sensible openings,
strike at these surely,
without any risk;
worry not about what he can do.[278]

If you want vengeance,
artfully break the four openings:
duplicate above,
mutate correctly below.
Certainly I say this:
no master defends himself without danger.
If this you perceive,
he cannot make his blows.[279]

Cut out Crookedly and deftly,
cast the point to the hands.[280]

He who throws Crookedly well
with a step, he will defeat cuts.[281]

Cut Crookedly to the flat
of the masters, if you want to weaken them.[282]

When it clashes above
stand off, this I shall praise.[283]

Do not go Crookedly, cut short,
then show changing-through.[284]

When his Crooked cut foils you,
the noble war confuses him,
so that he truthfully knows not
where he shall be without danger.[285]

---

[276] Ibid., 20v-21r.
[277] Ibid., 22r.
[278] Ibid., 22v.
[279] Ibid., 23r.
[280] Ibid., 24v.
[281] Ibid., 25r.
[282] Ibid., 25v.
[283] Ibid.
[284] Ibid., 26r.
[285] Ibid., 26v.

The Cross strike takes away
that which comes from above.[286]

Cross with the "strong";
mark your work well with this.[287]

Cross to the Plough,
and strike hard to the Ox.[288]

He who Crosses well
with a spring, threatens the head.[289]

He who does a good feint,
strikes from below how he wishes.[290]

The turner subdues,
runs through and grapples.
Take the elbow certainly,
spring against him in the balance.[291]

Feint twice to
hit him. Then do the slice.[292]

Continue doubly with this,
step to the left and do not be slow.[293]

The Squinter counters
that which a buffalo cuts or thrusts.
That which threatens with changing
is robbed by the Squinter.[294]

Squint when he comes close to you;
change through, into his face.[295]

Squint to the point
and take his neck without fear.[296]

Squint to the head above
and the hands you will hurt.[297]

The Parter
threatens the face.[298]

---

[286] Ibid., 27r.
[287] Ibid., 27v.
[288] Ibid., 28v.
[289] Ibid., 29v.
[290] Ibid.
[291] Ibid., 30r.
[292] Ibid., 30v.
[293] Ibid., 30v.
[294] Ibid., 31r.
[295] Ibid., 31v.
[296] Ibid., 32r.
[297] Ibid., 32v.
[298] Ibid.

With the turning,
the breast is threatened swiftly.[299]

That which comes from him,
the Crown takes away.[300]

Slice through the Crown,
so you defeat this guard quickly.
Press with the sword,
pull away with a slice.[301]

Four postures alone
you will hold, and curse the common.
"Ox", "Plough", "Fool", "From the Roof ",
with these do not be unfamiliar.[302]

There are four displacements,
that also hurt the postures.
For the displacements protect you;
but if it happens to you, it will trouble you.[303]

If you are displaced
and if it comes to this,
hear what I advise:
go up, strike quickly and with haste.[304]

Set on to the four ends,
remain upon them, if you want to learn to finish.[305]

Learn to follow after
twice, or cut into the defence.[306]

Two outer takings.
Your work shall then begin.
And test the threats,
if they are weak or strong.[307]

Learn to Feel.
"Instantly" - this word cuts sharply.[308]

Follow after twice,
hit him and do the "old slice" as well.[309]

---

[299] Ibid., 33r.
[300] Ibid.
[301] Ibid., 33v.
[302] Ibid., 33v-34r.
[303] Ibid., 34v-35r.
[304] Ibid., 35v.
[305] Ibid., 36r.
[306] Ibid., 36v.
[307] Ibid., 37v.
[308] Ibid., 38r.
[309] Ibid., 39r.

He who aims below,
overrun him, he will be shamed.
When it clashes above,
be strong: that I will praise.
Make your work
or press hard twice.[310]

Learn to set aside,
cripple cuts and thrusts with skill.
That which is thrust against you,
meet it with your point and break it.
From both sides
always step if you wish to strike.[311]
Learn to change-through
from both sides, hurt him with thrusts.
He who binds with you
the changing-through finds him quickly.[312]

Step close in the bind,
the pull lets you find good hits.
Pull! Meet him, then pull again.
Find your work: then give pain.
Pull in all exchanges
against the masters, if you want to trick them.[313]

Run-through! Let it hang
with the pommel, seize if you want to grapple.
When strength is against you:
remember to run-through.[314]

Slice off from the hard blows,
from below give him both threats.
Four are the slices,
two below and two above.[315]

Wind the edge,
to suppress, press the hands.[316]

Know two hangings
from each hand, from the ground.
In all movements:
strikes, thrusts, postures – weak or hard.[317]

[310] Ibid., 39v.
[311] Ibid., 40r.
[312] Ibid., 41r.
[313] Ibid., 41r-41v.
[314] Ibid., 42r.
[315] Ibid., 44v.
[316] Ibid., 46r.
[317] Ibid., 46r-46v.

Make the speaking window:
stand freely, see what he does.
Strike in, thus he snaps.
See if he withdraws before you,
truly I say this to you:
no man can defend himself without danger!
If you have understood this correctly,
he cannot make his blows.[318]

He who acts well and counters correctly,
who understands completely,
and who breaks apart
everything with the three wounders,
who uses the hangers well and correctly,
and winds when these occur,
with eight windings;
who considers correctly
that each of
the windings are threefold, so I mean
that there are twenty
and four, when counted
from both sides.
Learn the eight windings with steps.
And test the threats
for nothing else: just weak or hard.[319]

[318] Ibid., 47r.
[319] Ibid., 124v.

Appendix B: Suggested Reading List

For students who are eager to learn more about the discipline of the German longsword, the Academy of Historical Arts recommends the following sources for further study. The sources should be read in the following order, so as to maximise one's understanding of the material therein. There are some translations available online free of charge, or there are professionally researched and published translations that can be bought via online bookstores or can be purchased directly from the publishers in some cases.

Codex Hs.3227a, aka the Codex Döbringer

This treatise contains only text, there are no images, but the text is both descriptive and evocative. This is one of the best sources for a student who wishes to develop a feel for the flavour of the discipline.

It should not be used as a "how to" manual. It does not contain much information about how to do the various techniques, and sometimes the descriptions can be frustratingly vague and cryptic. What it does manage to do extremely well is to provide a general overview of the system. It introduces all the various principles, it shows how ideas and concepts and techniques all fit together.

Even advanced students may benefit from reading this manuscript; there is always some new concept to understand, no matter how often the text is read.

The most accessible translation of this source was written by David Lindholm, and is available free of charge from several websites online. A brief online search and you will find it available for download.

MS Dresd. C487, aka the Codex Ringeck

This is another textual manuscript without any images, and in a similar vein to the Codex Döbringer, the text is clear and interesting. However, this source contains much more information about how to do the various techniques and the scenarios where the techniques should be used.

Once you have gained an understanding of the system from the Codex Döbringer, the Codex Ringeck is the next source that you should read. It will build upon the general overview offered by the previous treatise and will flesh out your knowledge of the different techniques.

An English translation of this source was written by Keith Farrell, and is available free of charge online from the Academy of Historical Arts website.

Codex 44.A.8, aka the _Codex Danzig_

This manuscript is very similar to the _Codex Ringeck_, but the explanations are slightly different in places. This treatise could be read instead of the _Codex Ringeck_ and it would still complement the _Codex Döbringer_. However, reading both this treatise and Ringeck's treatise will help to solidify what you know about the different techniques and scenarios in the system, and can lead to quite valuable insights and ideas.

The best translation of this source was written by Christian Tobler and has been published in his book _In St George's Name_.

MS Thott.290.2º, by Hans Talhoffer

Talhoffer is one of the best-known medieval fencing masters. His books have been reprinted regularly throughout the centuries and many modern practitioners will have begun their studies of historical fencing by looking at one of Talhoffer's books.

Unfortunately, his books are not very helpful when compared with sources like the _Codex Ringeck_ or the _Codex Döbringer_, and reading them without an understanding of the complete system can lead to developing some very strange ideas about the techniques contained within. However, by reading this book after the three sources advised previously, you will be able to place the techniques and ideas in the context of the entire system.

This particular book by Talhoffer contains some very interesting information about the context of judicial duels and how people prepared for duels. It also contains techniques for several different styles of fighting and a copy of the _Bellifortis_, a treatise illustrating all kinds of siege equipment and other bizarre martial technology.

The best translation of this source was written by Jeffrey Hull, and is available free of charge from various websites online. A brief Google search and you will find it available for download.

Codex icon.394a, by Hans Talhoffer

This is another manuscript by Hans Talhoffer, probably the most widely known of his works amongst modern practitioners. It is worth developing a familiarity with this source and trying to apply knowledge gained from the _Codex Döbringer_, _Codex Ringeck_ and _Codex Danzig_ to this cryptic set of illustrations.

The best way to investigate this source is to access it through the online Wiktenauer website.

Thorough Description of the Art of Combat, by Joachim Meyer

Joachim Meyer wrote a manual in 1570 containing information and advice that differs significantly from the earlier sources. However, it is worth investigating this later source to learn an alternative point of view about how fencing should be conducted.

Dr Jeffrey Forgeng wrote the best translation of this source, but unfortunately this book is out of print and very difficult to acquire. Another option is a translation of Meyer's earlier manuscript from 1560; it is a slightly different treatise, with slightly different information, but the gist does appear to be somewhat similar. Kevin Maurer has released a translation of the 1560 manuscript that is available free of charge online from the website of the Meyer Freifechter Guild.

The Wiktenauer

For further study, and indeed for any sort of study pertaining to German longsword, the Wiktenauer is a wonderful place to start looking for information. It hosts many transcriptions and translations from researchers around the world. It would not be an exaggeration to say that the Wiktenauer is probably the greatest resource in the world at the moment for students of the historical European martial arts.

http://wiktenauer.com/

Appendix C: Glossary of German Terms

Guards

Hut	-	guard
Vom Tag	-	high guard ("from the roof")
Ochs	-	ox guard
Pflug	-	plough guard
Alber	-	fool's guard
Henngenort	-	hanging guard
Underhangen	-	another term for the plough guard, in the bind
Oberhangen	-	another term for the ox guard, in the bind
Langenort	-	long point
Schrankhut	-	barrier guard
Eyseryn Porte	-	iron gate guard
Nebenhut	-	near guard
Wechselhut	-	change guard
Zornhut	-	wrath guard
Einhorn	-	unicorn guard
Kron	-	crown guard
Mittelhut	-	middle guard
Sprechfenster	-	speaking window, another term for long point
Brechfenster	-	window breaker

Strikes

Haw	-	a strike with an edge
Schlag	-	a strike with any part of the weapon
Ort	-	point or thrust
Zorn Ort	-	thrust of wrath
Oberhaw	-	strike from high to low
Underhaw	-	rising strike from underneath
Mittelhaw	-	horizontal strike across the middle
Sturtzhaw	-	plunging cut
Wechselhaw	-	changing cut
Donnerschlag	-	thunder strike, same as Mortschlag
Mortschlag	-	murder strike, same as Donnerschlag
Pfobenzagel	-	peacock's tail, while in long-point, turning your point in circles around the opponent's blade until you can find an opening

Openings

Blossen	-	openings
Zum Pflug Schlagen	-	striking towards the lower openings
Zum Ochs Schlagen	-	striking towards the higher openings

Distances

Zufechten	-	the "to-fight"
Krieg	-	the war, close combat in the bind
Edel Krieg	-	the noble war
Abzug	-	retreating, withdrawal

Miscellaneous Attacking Terms

Stosse	-	thrust
Schnitt	-	slice
Drei Wunder	-	the "three wounders": striking, thrusting and slicing
Drucken	-	pressing
Schutze	-	cover

Master Strikes

Meisterhaw	-	master strike
Verbognehew	-	secret strike
Zornhaw	-	wrath strike
Zwerhaw	-	cross strike
Schaitelhaw	-	parting strike
Schilhaw	-	squinting strike
Krumphaw	-	crooked strike
Vier Versetzen	-	the four displacements; the four master strikes that "break" an opponent's guard

Timings

Vor	-	the "before"
Nach	-	the "after"
Indes	-	the "instant"
Nachreissen	-	travelling after

Striking Concepts

Vorschlag	-	the first strike
Nachschlag	-	strikes thrown after the first strike
Duplieren	-	doubling; striking high from the bind
Mutieren	-	mutating; thrusting low from the bind
Durchwechsel	-	changing through
Durchlauffen	-	running through
Einlauffen	-	running in

Types of Fighting

Blossfechten	-	unarmoured fighting on foot
Harnischfechten	-	armoured combat on foot
Kampffechten	-	armoured combat on foot
Underhalten	-	pinning someone to the floor while grappling
Harnusche	-	armour

Binding and Winding

Binden	-	when two blades meet together
Winden	-	winding the blade in the bind
Hart	-	strong at the bind
Weich	-	weak at the bind
Veste	-	firm at the bind
Fühlen	-	feeling
Zucken	-	from the bind, twitch to withdraw the sword so that the other sword passes by safely, then strike freely to the head
Umbschlagen	-	striking round from the bind
Schnappen	-	snapping round from the bind

Defending

Versetzen	-	displacing a technique
Uberlauffen	-	reaching over
Abesneit	-	cutting away
Veller	-	feinting
Abesetzen	-	parry, set aside
Abelecken	-	parry, set aside
Abweisest	-	parry, set aside

Motion

Motus	-	motion
Frequens Motus	-	constant motion
Spronge / Spring	-	leap / spring
Umbeschreiten	-	stepping around
Abe und Zutreten	-	stepping in and out

Grappling

Greiffen	-	grab /grip / close / closing
Krieg	-	close combat
Halb Schwerte	-	half sword
Ringen	-	wrestling
Ringen am Schwert	-	a specific branch of wrestling, in which one wrestles while still "at" the sword

Parts of the Sword

Ort	-	point
Schneide	-	edge
Kurze Schneide	-	short edge
Lange Schneide	-	long edge
Hohlkehle	-	fuller
Klinge	-	blade
Gehilze	-	hilt
Klos	-	pommel
Heft	-	grip
Schwert	-	sword
Starke	-	strong of the sword, half closest to hilt
Schwech	-	weak of the sword, half furthest from hilt
Schilt	-	shield of the sword, at the base of the blade

Bibliography

Websites:

http://www.hammaborg.de/en/fechtbuecher/start.php
http://www.middleages.hu/english/martialarts/treatise_database.php
http://wiktenauer.com/wiki/Main_Page
http://talhoffer.wordpress.com/
http://www.eskirmology.co.uk/
http://www.fioredeiliberi.org/phpBB3/index.php
http://hemaalliance.com/discussion/
http://www.hemac.org/
http://www.wmacoalition.com/forum/
http://www.swordforum.com/
http://www.hroarr.com/
http://historical-academy.co.uk/blog/
http://www.thearma.org/
http://boxwrestlefence.com/
http://talhoffer.blogspot.co.uk/
http://www.worksofrichardmarsden.com/
http://iceweasel.org/lmod_analysis.html

Videos:

YouTube Channel: TheRealGladiatores
http://www.youtube.com/user/TheRealGladiatores

    Fechten mit dem langen Schwert
    http://www.youtube.com/watch?v=Kj4Ng6DBfrg

    Some long sword fencing pieces after Danzig & Ringeck
    http://www.youtube.com/watch?v=HC5FIyfI8TA

    Fencing with five different medieval weapons
    http://www.youtube.com/watch?v=-TzdtyMC7ek

YouTube Channel: Dierk Hagedorn
http://www.youtube.com/user/DierkHagedorn

    Hammaborg: Longsword Techniques from Codex Wallerstein Pt. 1/7
    http://www.youtube.com/watch?v=WH8PtN1HCoE

    Hammaborg: Longsword Techniques from Codex Wallerstein Pt. 2/7
    http://www.youtube.com/watch?v=VbmF6UCFuyo

    Hammaborg: Longsword Techniques from Codex Wallerstein Pt. 3/7
    http://www.youtube.com/watch?v=wXzTDQMK0bw

Hammaborg: Longsword Techniques from Codex Wallerstein Pt. 4/7
http://www.youtube.com/watch?v=58PVzj6AWuc

Hammaborg: Longsword Techniques from Codex Wallerstein Pt. 5/7
http://www.youtube.com/watch?v=j214bzJ5S00

Hammaborg: Longsword Techniques from Codex Wallerstein Pt. 6/7
http://www.youtube.com/watch?v=nqaOMFuDpNI

Hammaborg: Longsword Techniques from Codex Wallerstein Pt. 7/7
http://www.youtube.com/watch?v=YKW6ZB8aKB8

Hammaborg - Longsword Techniques (Pt. 1/8): Peter Falkner Manuscript
http://www.youtube.com/watch?v=T5PXsznTHbQ

Hammaborg - Longsword Techniques (Pt. 2/8): Peter Falkner Manuscript
http://www.youtube.com/watch?v=gOse-yyHIwc

Hammaborg - Longsword Techniques (Pt. 3/8): Peter Falkner Manuscript
http://www.youtube.com/watch?v=aFLqe353Z-4

Hammaborg - Longsword Techniques (Pt. 4/8): Peter Falkner Manuscript
http://www.youtube.com/watch?v=PBd2ZTfeVkU

Hammaborg - Longsword Techniques (Pt. 5/8): Peter Falkner Manuscript
http://www.youtube.com/watch?v=2lPTkOmrZBU

Hammaborg - Longsword Techniques (Pt. 6/8): Peter Falkner Manuscript
http://www.youtube.com/watch?v=HyXyyFtDCcE

Hammaborg - Longsword Techniques (Pt. 7/8): Peter Falkner Manuscript
http://www.youtube.com/watch?v=tbJQvt5VzOQ

Hammaborg - Longsword Techniques (Pt. 8/8): Peter Falkner Manuscript
http://www.youtube.com/watch?v=Bkr7LaVIVVU

The Reversed Hand in Codex Wallerstein (1/2)
http://www.youtube.com/watch?v=QOamzdO-th0

The Reversed Hand in Codex Wallerstein (2/2)
http://www.youtube.com/watch?v=odAleRpD5hY

The Reversed Hand in Peter Falkner (KK 5012)
http://www.youtube.com/watch?v=94p1R6RZ50o

YouTube Channel: Anton Kohutovic
http://www.youtube.com/user/kohutovic

Zornhau training - Lichtenauers longsword techniques
http://www.youtube.com/watch?v=mjT4JepA-Vc

Zwerchhau, absetzen, nachreissen - longsword techniques training
http://www.youtube.com/watch?v=ln94E9AGYTc

YouTube Channel: NYHFA
http://www.youtube.com/user/NYHFA

NYHFA Advanced Cutting Curriculum: Combination Cuts
http://www.youtube.com/watch?v=n4ucqArlmpk

NYHFA Advanced Cutting Curriculum Part 2: Half Cuts
http://www.youtube.com/watch?v=C9FxOatYP0s

Cutting with the German Longsword
http://www.youtube.com/watch?v=HNEBpu8eDsU

YouTube Channel: ryrlen
http://www.youtube.com/user/ryrlen

GHFS Longsword show on KMD2010
http://www.youtube.com/watch?v=Ki-8HK1RD1w

YouTube Channel: ZornhauEV
http://www.youtube.com/user/ZornhauEV

Longsword-Techniques by Zornhau, Offenbach/Germany
http://www.youtube.com/watch?v=Y3DhjFUOG6Y

YouTube Channel: Bratislavsky sermiarsky spolok
http://www.youtube.com/user/johnmeadowcourt

Schermus Pictus
http://www.youtube.com/watch?v=-82cajZi70s

Schielhau Krumphau
http://www.youtube.com/watch?v=VIKMPIFJkzk

Lichtenawer's Kunst des Fechtens
http://www.youtube.com/watch?v=nKEdcCSz_8c

Summer longsword pieces HD
http://www.youtube.com/watch?v=8SoCRiETBsE

Lichtenauer fencing practice
http://www.youtube.com/watch?v=ByxdpgWS9GU

YouTube Channel: MEMAG
http://www.youtube.com/user/memag

The Zornhau (Wrath Hew)
http://www.youtube.com/watch?v=6ainzFa7mHc

The Schielhau "Squinting Hew"
http://www.youtube.com/watch?v=uhTY5cLB9ZU

The Krumphau
http://www.youtube.com/watch?v=bulXaHzNJ9Q

The Zwerchhau (Outdated Interpretations)
http://www.youtube.com/watch?v=oS-fFZKunzE

Codex Wallerstein Longsword Section
http://www.youtube.com/watch?v=io9I4wZ8FZk

Geselle Longsword Syllabus
http://www.youtube.com/watch?v=aLSn0JAQsFg

YouTube Channel: DerAltenFechter
http://www.youtube.com/user/DerAltenFechter

MKDF Cutting Drills - Matt Galas's Drills
http://www.youtube.com/watch?v=x9whFajLZnU

MKDF Cutting Drill - Shoulders and Thighs
http://www.youtube.com/watch?v=-N_1K3V4TVo

MKDF Shielhau 2011
http://www.youtube.com/watch?v=I_hph7_8MHc

MKDF Triangle/Zornhau-ort drill
http://www.youtube.com/watch?v=mF6H2KxXOZE

YouTube Channel: avalongliwice
http://www.youtube.com/user/avalongliwice

Vectir - Schielhaw (eng)
http://www.youtube.com/watch?v=h8U1LG27cVc

Vectir - ranges(eng)
http://www.youtube.com/watch?v=Z6h-NuyCFgU

Vectir - Absetzen(eng)
http://www.youtube.com/watch?v=iPpZIdP5kBY

YouTube Channel: ArtesBelli
http://www.youtube.com/user/ArtesBelli

The flourish of the Döbringer codex HS 3227a by Keith Farrell
http://www.youtube.com/watch?v=AoK8nvv0nZo

Facsimiles / Transcriptions / Translations:

Anonymous. *Bayeux Tapestry*, c.1070. Digitally reproduced by Glen Ray Crack, http://hastings1066.com/baythumb.shtml

Anonymous. *Maciejowski Bible*, c.1250. Digitally reproduced by Medieval Tymes, http://www.medievaltymes.com/courtyard/maciejowski_bible.htm

Anonymous. *MS I.33*, c.1290. Digitally reproduced by Dieter Bachmann, http://freywild.ch/i33/i33en.html

Anonymous. *Cod.HS.3227a or Hanko Döbringer Fechtbüch from 1389*, c.1389. Transcribed and translated by David Lindholm, 2005. http://www.ghfs.se/images/manualer/langsvaerd/Dobringer_A5_sidebyside.pdf

Anonymous. *MS KK5013*, 1430. Hosted by HROARR, http://www.hroarr.com/manuals/liechtenauer/1400(c)%20-%20Gladiatoria%20-%20Vienna.zip

Anonymous. *Codex 44.A.8*, 1452. Hosted by the Wiktenauer, http://wiktenauer.com/wiki/Codex_Danzig_(Cod.44.A.8)

Anonymous. *Codex I.6.4º.2*, 1470. Digitally reproduced by the Universitätsbibliothek Augsburg, http://media.bibliothek.uni-augsburg.de/node?cunfold=82373&dir=82373&id=82373

Anonymous. *MS M.I.29*, 1479. Transcribed by Dierk Hagedorn, translated by Beatrix Knoll, hosted by the Wiktenauer, http://wiktenauer.com/wiki/Codex_Speyer_%28MS_M.I.29%29

Anonymous. *MS Best.7020*, c.1500s. Translated by James Wallhausen, 2011. http://paleo.eskirmology.co.uk/best-7020-Fechtbüch/

Anonymous. *The Glasgow Fechtbüch*, 1508. Hosted by the Wiktenauer, http://wiktenauer.com/wiki/Glasgow_Fechtbuch_(MS_E.1939.65.341)

Anonymous. *MS Germ.Quart.2020; aka the Goliath Fechtbüch*, 1515. Translated by Michael Rasmusson, 2004. Hosted by the Wiktenauer, http://wiktenauer.com/wiki/Goliath

Breu, Jörg. *Codex I.6.2º.4*, 1545. Digitally reproduced by the Universitätsbibliothek Augsburg, http://media.bibliothek.uni-augsburg.de/node?cfold=82166&dir=82166&id=82166

Falkner, Peter. *MS KK5012*, 1495. Hosted by the WikiMedia Foundation, http://commons.wikimedia.org/

Grassi, Giacomo di. *His True Arte of Defence*, 1594. Digitally reproduced by the Raymond J. Lord Collection, http://www.umass.edu/renaissance/lord/pdfs/DiGrassi_1594.pdf

Hutter, Jörg Wilhalm. *CGM 3711*, 1523. Digitally reproduced by the Bayerische StaatsBibliothek,
http://daten.digitale-sammlungen.de/0006/bsb00064546/images/index.html

Hutter, Jörg Wilhalm. *Codex I.6.2º.2*, 1523. Digitally reproduced by the Universitätsbibliothek Augsburg,
http://media.bibliothek.uni-augsburg.de/node?id=81795&unfold=81795

Kal, Paulus. *MS 1825*, 1458. Digitally reproduced by the Biblioteca Universitaria,
http://hroarr.com/manuals/liechtenauer/Paulus%20Kal%20MS1825.zip

Kal, Paulus. *Codex Germ.1507*, 1470. Digitally reproduced by the Bayerische StaatsBibliothek,
http://daten.digitale-sammlungen.de/0000/bsb00001840/images/index.html

Kal, Paulus. *Codex S 554*, 1506. Hosted by the Wiktenauer,
http://wiktenauer.com/wiki/1500s_-_Solothurner_Fechtbüch_%28Cod.S.554%29

Lew, Jud. *Codex I.6.4º.3*, 1450. Transcribed by Dierk Hagedorn, 2009.
http://www.hammaborg.de/en/transkriptionen/jude_lew/index.php

Liberi, Fiore dei. *Fior de Battaglia*, 1410. Translated and hosted by The Exiles, 2008.
http://www.the-exiles.org.uk/fioreproject/Project.htm

Mair, Paulus. *MS Dresd. C93*, 1542. Digitally reproduced by the Sächsische Landesbibliothek,
http://digital.slub-dresden.de/werkansicht/dlf/7522/1/

Mair, Paulus. *Codex icon.393*, 1550. Digitally reproduced by the Bayerische StaatsBibliothek,
http://daten.digitale-sammlungen.de/0000/bsb00006570/images/index.html

Medel, Hans. *Codex I.6.2º.5*, 1539. Digitally reproduced by the Universitätsbibliothek Augsburg, http://media.bibliothek.uni-augsburg.de/node?id=47755

Meyer, Joachim. *MS A.4º.2*, 1560. Hosted by HROARR,
http://hroarr.com/manuals/liechtenauer/joachim-meyer-1560.pdf

Meyer, Joachim. *MS A.4º.2*, 1560. Translated by Kevin Maurer, 2012.
https://sites.google.com/site/jochimmeyer1560/

Meyer, Joachim. *Gründtliche Beschreibung der Kunst des Fechtens*, 1570. Translated by Michael Rasmusson, 2002. Hosted by the Wiktenauer,
http://wiktenauer.com/wiki/Meyer

Meyer, Joachim. *Gründtliche Beschreibung der Kunst des Fechtens*, 1570. Digitally reproduced by the Bayerische StaatsBibliothek, http://nbn-resolving.de/urn:nbn:de:bvb:12-bsb00024580-2

Meyer, Joachim. *Gründtliche Beschreibung der Kunst des Fechtens*, 1600. Digitally reproduced by the Raymond J. Lord Collection, http://www.umass.edu/renaissance/lord/pdfs/Meyer_1600.pdf

Meyer, Joachim. *Gründtliche Beschreibung der Kunst des Fechtens*, 1600. Digitally reproduced by the Bayerische StaatsBibliothek, http://nbn-resolving.de/urn:nbn:de:bvb:12-bsb00024583-8

Paurñfeyndt, Andre. *Ergrundung Ritterlicher Kunst der Fechterey*, 1516. MS E.1939.65.341, held by the Glasgow Museums.

Ringeck, Sigmund ain. *Master Sigmund Ringeck's Commentaries on Johann Liechtenauer's Fechtbüch - c. 1389 to 1440*, c.1510. Transcribed by Christoph Kaindel, translated by Joerg Bellighausen, edited by John Clements, 2003. http://www.thearma.org/Manuals/Ringeck.htm

Ringeck, Sigmund ain. *Dresd. C487 'Ringeck'*, c.1510. Transcribed by Andreas Engström, 2008. http://www.ghfs.se/images/manualer/langsvaerd/Ringeck%20Faksimil%201.1.pdf

Ringeck, Sigmund ain. *Ringeck 1.3*, c.1510. Translated by Andreas Engström, 2008. http://www.ghfs.se/images/manualer/langsvaerd/Ringeck%201.3.pdf

Ringeck, Sigmund ain. *Ringeck Longsword*, c.1510. Translated by Keith Farrell, 2011. http://www.historical-academy.co.uk/files/research/keith-farrell/Ringeck%20Longsword.pdf

Sutor, Jakob. *New Künstliches Fechtbuch*, 1612. Digitally reproduced by Peter Valentine, http://www.thearma.org/pdf/JakobSutor.pdf

Sutor, Jakob. *New Künstliches Fechtbuch*, 1612. Translated by Keith P. Myers, 2010. http://freifechter.com/sutorian.pdf

Talhoffer, Hans. *MS Thott.290.2º*, 1459. Transcribed, translated and with commentary by Jeffrey Hull, 2006. http://www.thearma.org/pdf/Fight-Earnestly.pdf

Talhoffer, Hans. *Codex icon.394a*, 1467. Hosted by the WikiMedia Foundation, http://commons.wikimedia.org/

Books:

Anglo, Syndey. *The Martial Arts of Renaissance Europe.* Yale University Press, 2000.

Blair, Claude. *European Armour circa 1066 to circa 1700.* B.T. Bonanza, 1957.

Clements, John. *Medieval Swordsmanship.* Paladin Press, 1998.

Clements, John and Jeffrey Hull (eds). *Masters of Medieval and Renaissance Martial Arts: Rediscovering the Western Combat Heritage.* Paladin Press, 2008.

Edge, David and John Miles Paddock. *Arms and Armour of the Medieval Knight.* Bison Books, 1988.

Forgeng, Jeffrey. *The Medieval Art of Swordsmanship: A Facsimile and Translation of the World's Oldest Personal Combat Treatise.* Chivalry Bookshelf, 2004.

Forgeng, Jeffrey. *The Art of Combat: A German Martial Arts Treatise of 1570.* Palgrave MacMillan, 2006.

Gravett, Christopher. *Knight: Noble Warrior of England 1200-1600.* Osprey Publishing, 2008.

Hull, Jeffrey, Monika Maziarz and Grzegorz Żabiński. *Knightly Dueling: The Fighting Arts of German Chivalry.* Paladin Press, 2008.

Knight, David James and Brian Hunt. *Polearms of Paulus Hector Mair.* Sycamore Island Books, 2008.

Lindholm, David. *Sigmund Ringeck's "Knightly Art of the Longsword".* Paladin Press, 2003.

Oakeshott, Ewart. *Records of the Medieval Sword.* The Boydell Press, 1991.

Oakeshott, Ewart. *The Sword in the Age of Chivalry.* The Boydell Press, 2010.

Pearlman, Steven. *Book of Martial Power.* The Overlook Press, 2008.

Rector, Mark. *Medieval Combat.* London: Greenhill Books, 2000.

Tobler, Christian. *Fighting with the German Longsword.* Chivalry Bookshelf, 2004.

Tobler, Christian. *In Service of the Duke.* Chivalry Bookshelf, 2006.

Tobler, Christian. *In Saint Georges Name: An Anthology of Medieval German Fighting Arts.* Freelance Academy Press, 2010.

Tobler, Christian. *Captain of the Guild: Master Peter Falkner's Art of Knightly Defense.* Freelance Academy Press, 2011.

Wagner, Paul and Stephen Hand. *Medieval Sword and Shield: The Combat System of Royal Armouries MS I.33.* Chivalry Bookshelf, 2003.

Wallhausen, James. *Knightly Martial Arts.* Lulu.com, 2010.

Windsor, Guy. *The Swordsman's Companion: Modern Training Manual for Medieval Longsword.* Chivalry Bookshelf, 2004.

Żabiński, Grzegorz and Bartlomiej Walczak. *Codex Wallerstein: A Medieval Fighting Book from the Fifteenth Century on the Longsword, Falchion, Dagger, and Wrestling.* Paladin Press, 2002.

Żabiński, Grzegorz. *The Longsword Teachings of Master Liechtenauer. The Early Sixteenth Century Swordsmanship Comments in the "Goliath" Manuscript.* Adam Marshall, 2010.

Theses and Journal Articles:

Clements, John. "The Humanist Component within Renaissance Martial Arts Teachings" *IDO MOVEMENT FOR CULTURE, Journal of Martial Arts Anthropology* 11, no. 2 (2011): 32-37.

Farrell, Keith. "The pedagogical skill of Andre Lignitzer, a 15th century fencing master" *Katsujinken, a Sword Arts Journal* 5, (2013): 12-15.

Hester, James. "Real Men Read Poetry: Instructional Verse in 14th-century Fight Manuals" *Arms & Armour* 6, no. 2 (2009): 175-183.

Kerr, Ben. "Tournament: Martial Training or Elaborate Game?" MA(Hons) diss., University of Glasgow, 2009.

Moffat, Ralph. "The Manner of Arming Knights for the Tourney: A Re-Interpretation of an Important Early 14th-Century Arming Treatise" *Arms & Armour* 7, no. 1 (2010): 5-29.

Pelsmaeker, Sebastian. "Weapons of Princes, Weapons of War? An experimental analysis of pattern-welded swords from northwestern Europe, 400-100AD." MA diss., University of Groningen, 2010.

Walczak, Bartłomiej. "The Importance of Studying the Fechtbücher" *Journal of Western Martial Art,* (2009): http://ejmas.com/jwma/articles/2002/jwmaart_walczak_0102.htm

Walczak, Bartłomiej. "Bringing Lost Teachings Back to Life - A Proposed Method for Interpretation of Medieval and Renaissance Fencing Manuals" *IDO MOVEMENT FOR CULTURE, Journal of Martial Arts Anthropology* 11, no. 2 (2011): 38-46.

Essays:

Amberger, Christopher. "The Death of History: Historic European fighting arts in the Mis-information Age." The Secret History of the Sword, 2006. http://web.archive.org/web/20060518155508/http://swordhistory.com/excerpts/masters.html

Cartier, Mike. "The Art of Control." Meyer Frei Fechter Guild 2011. http://freifechter.com/TheArtofControl_fechtschulemanifesto.pdf

Clements, John. "Scale, Volta, and Key." The ARMA, 2010. http://www.thearma.org/VoltaKeyandScale.htm

Edelson, Michael. "Cutting with the Longsword." New York Historical Fencing Association, 2010. http://newyorklongsword.com/articles/cm.pdf

Edelson, Michael. "Western martial Arts Bouting: Recognizing and Dealing with Artifacts in Free Play." New York Historical Fencing Association, 2009. http://newyorklongsword.com/articles/WMAB.pdf

Galas, Matt. "Documenting One-Handed Attacks." Western Martial Arts Coalition, 2010. http://www.wmacoalition.com/forum/viewtopic.php?f=2&t=626

Galas, Matt. "The Notion of a 'Real Fight'." Western Martial Arts Coalition, 2010. http://www.wmacoalition.com/forum/viewtopic.php?f=2&t=659

Galas, Matt. "On the After-Blow." Western Martial Arts Coalition, 2010. http://www.wmacoalition.com/forum/viewtopic.php?f=2&t=611

Galas, Matt. "Historical Rule-Sets." Western Martial Arts Coalition, 2010. http://www.wmacoalition.com/forum/viewtopic.php?f=2&t=666

Galas, Matt. "Tournament Formats for HEMA." Western Martial Arts Coalition, 2010. http://www.wmacoalition.com/forum/viewtopic.php?f=2&t=669

Galas, Matt. "On the Value of Tournaments." Western Martial Arts Coalition, 2010. http://www.wmacoalition.com/forum/viewtopic.php?f=2&t=542

Galas, Matt. "Training to Avoid Double Hits." Western Martial Arts Coalition, 2010. http://www.wmacoalition.com/forum/viewtopic.php?f=2&t=461

Galas, Matt. "The Problem of the Double Hit." Western Martial Arts Coalition, 2010. http://www.wmacoalition.com/forum/viewtopic.php?f=2&t=462

Hull, Jeffrey. "Fight-Book Clues to Quality and Build of Knightly Weaponry." The ARMA, 2007. http://www.thearma.org/essays/quality-and-build.html

Hull, Jeffrey. "Döbringer Longsword Flourish." HEMA Alliance, 2010. http://www.hemaalliance.com/documents/Dobringer.Longsword.Flourish.pdf

Hull, Jeffrey. "Early European Longswords, Evidence of Form and Function." Academia.edu, 2012. http://www.academia.edu/2331258/Early_European_Longswords_Evidence_of_Form_and_Function

Hull, Jeffrey. "Inthereof: the Tactical Key to German Fencing." Academia.edu, 2012. http://www.academia.edu/2331274/Inthereof_the_Tactical_Key_to_German_Fencing

Hull, Jeffrey. "Mass in Medieval German Fighting Arts." Academia.edu, 2012. www.academia.edu/2331263/Mass_in_Medieval_German_Fighting_Arts

Knight, Hugh. "Some Observations on the Zornhau." Schlachtschule, 2009. http://www.schlachtschule.org/instruction/OntheZornhau.pdf

Page, Drew. "Introduction to Johannes Liechtenauer and His Combat System." Fursantiago, 2008. http://fursantiago.timduru.org/esgrima/Liechtenauer.pdf

Tobler, Christian. "In Defense of Peter von Danzig." Freelance Academy Press, 2010. http://www.freelanceacademypress.com/vondanzigdefense.aspx

Vanslambrouck, Christopher. "The Life and Work of Joachim Meyer." Meyer Frei Fechter Guild, 2010. http://freifechter.com/joachim_meyer.cfm

Blog Articles:

Bourdas, Alex. "Over Applying Liechtenauer's Principles." *Encased in Steel*, 2011. http://historical-academy.co.uk/blog/2011/03/11/43/

Bourdas, Alex. "A Perfect Length." *Encased in Steel*, 2011. http://historical-academy.co.uk/blog/2011/06/24/a-perfect-length-2/

Bourdas, Alex. "A Perfect Length II: The Longsword." *Encased in Steel*, 2011. http://historical-academy.co.uk/blog/2011/07/29/a-perfect-length-ii-the-longsword/

Bourdas, Alex. "Fitness for HEMA Part I: Cardio." *Encased in Steel*, 2011. http://historical-academy.co.uk/blog/2011/08/26/fitness-for-hema-part-i-cardio/

Bourdas, Alex. "Fitness for HEMA Part II: Strength Training." *Encased in Steel*, 2011. http://historical-academy.co.uk/blog/2011/09/02/fitness-for-hema-part-ii-strength-training/

Bourdas, Alex. "Simulators and HEMA Training." *Encased in Steel*, 2011. http://historical-academy.co.uk/blog/2011/11/18/simulators-and-hema-training/

Bourdas, Alex. "Principles and the Book of Martial Power." *Encased in Steel*, 2012. http://historical-academy.co.uk/blog/2012/05/18/principles-and-the-book-of-martial-power/

Bourdas, Alex. "Rushing forward, and besieging." *Encased in Steel*, 2012. http://historical-academy.co.uk/blog/2012/06/22/rushing-forward-and-besieging/

Bourdas, Alex. "The defensive advantage, the Vor, and the master strikes." *Encased in Steel*, 2012. http://historical-academy.co.uk/blog/2012/08/10/the-defensive-advantage-the-vor-and-the-master-strikes-2/

Bourdas, Alex. "Fuhlen, Indes and Managing Defensive and Offensive Advantages." *Encased in Steel*, 2012. http://historical-academy.co.uk/blog/2012/10/12/fuhlen-indes-and-managing-defensive-and-offensive-advantages/

Bourdas, Alex. "One Art of the Sword." *Encased in Steel*, 2012. http://historical-academy.co.uk/blog/2012/12/14/one-art-of-the-sword/

Bourdas, Alex. "The nervous system and isometrics." *Encased in Steel*, 2013. http://historical-academy.co.uk/blog/2013/01/18/the-nervous-system-and-isometrics/

Farrell, Keith. "Western Composers and Western Martial Arts." *Encased in Steel*, 2011. http://historical-academy.co.uk/blog/2011/04/29/western-composers-and-western-martial-arts/

Farrell, Keith. "What You Train is What You Do Under Pressure." *Encased in Steel*, 2011. http://historical-academy.co.uk/blog/2011/05/27/what-you-train-is-what-you-do-under-pressure/

Farrell, Keith. "Range, Distance and Timing in Sparring." *Encased in Steel*, 2011. http://historical-academy.co.uk/blog/2011/06/17/range-distance-and-timing-in-sparring/

Farrell, Keith. "Analysing Historical Sources." *Encased in Steel*, 2011. http://historical-academy.co.uk/blog/2011/09/17/analysing-historical-sources/

Farrell, Keith. "Environment and HEMA Training." *Encased in Steel*, 2011. http://historical-academy.co.uk/blog/2011/11/04/environment-and-hema-training/

Farrell, Keith. "Time Requirements in the Practice of Martial Arts." *Encased in Steel*, 2012. http://historical-academy.co.uk/blog/2012/08/03/time-requirements-in-the-practice-of-martial-arts/

Farrell, Keith. "Folia, Quires, Codices and Manuscripts - What Are They?" *Encased in Steel*, 2012. http://historical-academy.co.uk/blog/2012/03/23/folia-quires-codices-and-manuscripts-what-are-they/

Farrell, Keith. "Liechtenauer or a Derivative?" *Encased in Steel*, 2012. http://historical-academy.co.uk/blog/2012/05/04/liechtenauer-or-a-derivative/

Farrell, Keith. "Cutting concepts." *Encased in Steel*, 2012. http://historical-academy.co.uk/blog/2012/05/25/cutting-concepts/

Farrell, Keith. "Principles behind the 'Master Strikes'." *Encased in Steel*, 2012. http://historical-academy.co.uk/blog/2012/07/13/principles-behind-the-master-strikes/

Farrell, Keith. "What sort of protective gear is needed to practice martial arts?" *Encased in Steel*, 2012. http://historical-academy.co.uk/blog/2012/10/19/what-sort-of-protective-gear-is-needed-to-practice-martial-arts/

Farrell, Keith. "Comparing how swords were used - the importance of the hilt." *Encased in Steel*, 2012. http://historical-academy.co.uk/blog/2012/12/28/comparing-how-swords-were-used-%E2%80%93-the-importance-of-the-hilt/

Farrell, Keith. "For Beginners: Fiore or Liechtenauer?" *Encased in Steel*, 2013. http://historical-academy.co.uk/blog/2013/01/25/for-beginners-fiore-or-liechtenauer/

Farrell, Keith. "'Aggressive' vs 'Assertive' for Martial Arts." *Encased in Steel*, 2013. http://historical-academy.co.uk/blog/2013/02/11/aggressive-vs-assertive-for-martial-arts/

Farrell, Keith. "The danger of tournaments: hitting hard, or being unprepared to BE hit hard?" *Encased in Steel*, 2013. http://historical-academy.co.uk/blog/2013/03/01/the-danger-of-tournaments-hitting-hard-or-being-unprepared-to-be-hit-hard/

Fonda, Giorgio. "A journey through a technique: the Durchlauffen." *HROARR*, 2012. http://www.hroarr.com/a-journey-through-a-technique-the-durchlauffen/

Fritz, Falko. "Why Fight? The Objectives of Liechtenauer's Fencing." *HROARR*, 2012. http://www.hroarr.com/why-fight-the-objectives-of-liechtenauers-fencing/

Kerrigan, Hugh. "Were people shorter in the middle ages?" *Encased in Steel*, 2012. http://historical-academy.co.uk/blog/2012/07/27/were-people-shorter-in-the-middle-ages/

Knight, Hugh. "Are We Always Supposed to Attack First?" *The School of Battle*, 2008. http://talhoffer.blogspot.co.uk/2008/02/are-we-always-supposed-to-attack-first.html

Knight, Hugh. "Did Medieval Commoners Practice with Fighting Masters?" *The School of Battle*, 2008. http://talhoffer.blogspot.co.uk/2008/02/did-medieval-commoners-practice-with.html

Knight, Hugh. "From the Bind of the Zwerchau." *The School of Battle*, 2008. http://talhoffer.blogspot.co.uk/2008/02/from-bind-of-zwerchau.html

Knight, Hugh. "Attacks as Transitions From Guard to Guard." *The School of Battle*, 2008. http://talhoffer.blogspot.co.uk/2008/04/attacks-as-transitions-from-guard-to.html

Knight, Hugh. "What is a Master?" *The School of Battle*, 2008. http://talhoffer.blogspot.co.uk/2008/04/what-is-master.html

Knight, Hugh. "What Is Intent?" *The School of Battle*, 2008. http://talhoffer.blogspot.co.uk/2008/04/what-is-intent.html

Knight, Hugh. "Left vom Tag?" *The School of Battle*, 2008. http://talhoffer.blogspot.co.uk/2008/05/left-vom-tag.html

Knight, Hugh. "The drei Wunder." *The School of Battle*, 2008. http://talhoffer.blogspot.co.uk/2008/09/drei-wunder.html

Knight, Hugh. "Edge on Edge Contact." *The School of Battle*, 2009. http://talhoffer.blogspot.co.uk/2009/05/edge-on-edge-contact.html

Knight, Hugh. "What is vom Tag?" *The School of Battle*, 2009.
http://talhoffer.blogspot.co.uk/2009/05/what-is-vom-tag.html

Knight, Hugh. "Testing Yourself and Your Art." *The School of Battle*, 2009.
http://talhoffer.blogspot.co.uk/2009/05/testing-yourself-and-your-art.html

Knight, Hugh. "The Bind." *The School of Battle*, 2009.
http://talhoffer.blogspot.co.uk/2009/06/bind.html

Knight, Hugh. "On Mixing Styles." *The School of Battle*, 2009.
http://talhoffer.blogspot.co.uk/2009/07/on-mixing-styles.html

Knight, Hugh. "Are the Gladiatoria MSS Part of the Liechtenauer Canon?" *The School of Battle*, 2010.
http://talhoffer.blogspot.co.uk/2010/04/blog-post.html

Knight, Hugh. "Active Fühlen." *The School of Battle*, 2010.
http://talhoffer.blogspot.co.uk/2010/08/active-fuhlen.html

Knight, Hugh. "How Sharp Were Medieval Swords?" *The School of Battle*, 2011.
http://talhoffer.blogspot.co.uk/2011/05/how-sharp-were-medieval-swords.html

Knight, Hugh. "What is Kron?" *The School of Battle*, 2011.
http://talhoffer.blogspot.co.uk/2011/05/what-is-kron.html

Knight, Hugh. "The Four Oppositions." *The School of Battle*, 2012.
http://talhoffer.blogspot.co.uk/2012/07/four-oppositions.html

Kleinau, Jens Peter. "Off Measures?" *Hans Talhoffer – as seen by Jens P. Kleinau*, 2011. http://talhoffer.wordpress.com/2011/05/15/off-measures-2/

Kleinau, Jens Peter. "En Garde on Guards." *Hans Talhoffer – as seen by Jens P. Kleinau*, 2011. http://talhoffer.wordpress.com/2011/05/19/on-guard-enguarde/

Kleinau, Jens Peter. "Paulus Kal, a Schirrmeister." *Hans Talhoffer – as seen by Jens P. Kleinau*, 2011.
http://talhoffer.wordpress.com/2011/07/03/paulus-kal-a-schirrmeister/

Kleinau, Jens Peter. "Engineers and masters of warfare." *Hans Talhoffer – as seen by Jens P. Kleinau*, 2012.
http://talhoffer.wordpress.com/2011/07/07/engineers-and-masters-of-warfare/

Kleinau, Jens Peter. "Chronicle of the Fencing Guilds in Augsburg." *Hans Talhoffer – as seen by Jens P. Kleinau*, 2012.
http://talhoffer.wordpress.com/2012/04/25/chronicle-of-the-fencing-guilds-in-augsburg/

Kleinau, Jens Peter. "The definition of 'One step away'." *Hans Talhoffer – as seen by Jens P. Kleinau*, 2012.
http://talhoffer.wordpress.com/2012/05/07/the-definition-of-one-step-away/

Kleinau, Jens Peter. "Understanding Zufechten." *Hans Talhoffer – as seen by Jens P. Kleinau*, 2012.
http://talhoffer.wordpress.com/2012/05/07/understanding-zufechten/

Kleinau, Jens Peter. "The simplicity of the 'Vor'." *Hans Talhoffer – as seen by Jens P. Kleinau*, 2012.
http://talhoffer.wordpress.com/2012/05/16/the-simplicity-of-the-vor/

Kleinau, Jens Peter. "Active or Passive, and Double 'Vor'." *Hans Talhoffer – as seen by Jens P. Kleinau*, 2012.
http://talhoffer.wordpress.com/2012/05/16/active-or-passive-and-double-vor/

Morini, Andrea. "About the flat parry." *HROARR*, 2012.
http://www.hroarr.com/about-the-flat-parry/

Norling, Roger. "How do you grip a sword?" *HROARR*, 2011.
http://www.hroarr.com/how-do-you-grip-a-sword/

Norling, Roger. "How do you do the Vom Tag?" *HROARR*, 2011.
http://www.hroarr.com/how-do-you-do-the-vom-tag/

Norling, Roger. "Is there really a Left Vom Tag?" *HROARR*, 2011.
http://www.hroarr.com/is-there-really-a-left-vom-tag/

Norling, Roger. "Federschwert or a blunt longsword?"
http://www.hroarr.com/federschwert-or-a-blunt-longsword/

Norling, Roger. "How long should a longsword be?" *HROARR*, 2011.
http://www.hroarr.com/how-long-should-a-longsword-be/

Norling, Roger. "The tools for the job." *HROARR*, 2012.
http://www.hroarr.com/the-tools-for-the-job/

Norling, Roger. "The history of Joachim Meyer's fencing treatise to Otto von Solms." *HROARR*, 2012.
http://www.hroarr.com/the-history-of-joachim-meyers-treatise-to-von-solms/

Norling, Roger. "Doing what we are told or what we are taught? - Part 1." *HROARR*, 2012. http://www.hroarr.com/doing-what-we-are-told-or-what-we-are-taught/

Norling, Roger. "Heinrich Cornelius Agrippa, a fine student, black magician - and a Freyfechter?" *HROARR*, 2012.
http://www.hroarr.com/heinrich-cornelius-agrippa-a-fine-student-black-magician-and-a-freyfechter/

Norling, Roger. "The Rose and the Pentagram." *HROARR*, 2012.
http://www.hroarr.com/the-rose-and-the-pentagram/

Norling, Roger. "The Wreath or the Cash? On Tournament fighting." *HROARR*, 2012.
http://www.hroarr.com/the-wreath-or-the-cash-on-tournament-fighting/

Norling, Roger. "Remember Mair." *HROARR*, 2012.
http://www.hroarr.com/remember-mair/

Norling, Roger. "The WhatChaMaCallIt-Schwert." *HROARR*, 2013.
http://www.hroarr.com/the-feder-whatchamacallit/

Norling, Roger. "Meyer's Masters." *HROARR*, 2013.
http://www.hroarr.com/meyers-masters/

Pearce, Tinker. "The Rules of the Fight and Effective Training." *HROARR*, 2012.
http://www.hroarr.com/the-rules-of-the-fight-and-effective-training/

Vanslambrouck, Christopher. "The OODA Loop & HEMA." *HROARR*, 2012.
http://www.hroarr.com/the-ooda-loop-hema/